THE STORY OF
BADEN-POWELL

'The Wolf that never Sleeps'

HAROLD BEGBIE

1st WORLD
LIBRARY
Literary Society

The Story of Baden-Powell

Harold Begbie

© 1st World Library, 2006
PO Box 2211
Fairfield, IA 52556
www.1stworldlibrary.com
First Edition

LCCN: 2006936215

Softcover ISBN: 978-1-4218-3062-9
Hardcover ISBN: 978-1-4218-2962-3
eBook ISBN: 978-1-4218-3162-6

Purchase *"The Story of Baden-Powell"*
as a traditional bound book at:
www.1stWorldLibrary.com/purchase.asp?ISBN=978-1-4218-3062-9

1st World Library is a literary, educational organization
dedicated to:

- Creating a free internet library of downloadable ebooks

- Hosting writing competitions and offering book
publishing scholarships.

Interested in more 1st World Library books?
contact: literacy@1stworldlibrary.com
Check us out at: www.1stworldlibrary.com

1st World Library Literary Society

Giving Back to the World

"If you want to work on the core problem, it's early school literacy."

- James Barksdale, former CEO of Netscape

"No skill is more crucial to the future of a child, or to a democratic and prosperous society, than literacy."

- Los Angeles Times

Literacy... means far more than learning how to read and write... The aim is to transmit... knowledge and promote social participation."

- UNESCO

"Literacy is not a luxury, it is a right and a responsibility. If our world is to meet the challenges of the twenty-first century we must harness the energy and creativity of all our citizens."

- President Bill Clinton

"Parents should be encouraged to read to their children, and teachers should be equipped with all available techniques for teaching literacy, so the varying needs and capacities of individual kids can be taken into account."

- Hugh Mackay

"... A name and an example, which are at this hour inspiring hundreds of the youth of England...."

Southey's *Life of Nelson.*

To SMITH MAJOR

HONOURED SIR,

If amid the storm and stress of your academic career you find an hour's relaxation in perusing the pages of this book, all the travail that I have suffered in the making of it will be repaid a thousandfold. Throughout the quiet hours of many nights, when Morpheus has mercifully muzzled my youngest (a fine child, sir, but a female), I have bent over my littered desk driving a jibbing pen, comforted and encouraged simply and solely by the vision of my labour's object and attainment. I have seen at such moments the brink of a river, warm with the sun's rays, though sheltered in part by the rustling leaves of an alder, and thereon, sprawling at great ease, chin in the cups of the hand, stomach to earth, and toes tapping the sweet-smelling sod, your illustrious self—deep engrossed in my book. For this alone I have written. If, then, it was the prospect of thus pleasing you that sustained me in my task, to whom else can I more fittingly inscribe the fruits of my labour? Accept then, honoured sir, this work of your devoted servant, assured that, if the book wins your affection and leaves an ideal or two in the mind when you come regretfully upon "Finis," I shall smoke my pipe o' nights with greater pleasure and content-ment than ever I have done since I ventured the task of sketching my gallant hero's adventurous career.

I have the honour to be, sir,
Your most humble and obedient servant,
THE AUTHOR.
WEYBRIDGE, *April 1900.*

CONTENTS

CHAPTER I

AN INTRODUCTORY FRAGMENT ON NO ACCOUNT TO BE SKIPPED

You will be the first to grant me, honoured sir, that after earnestness of purpose, that is to say "keenness," there is no quality of the mind so essential to the even-balance as humour. The schoolmaster without this humanising virtue never yet won your love and admiration, and to miss your affection and loyalty is to lose one of life's chiefest delights. You are as quick to detect the humbug who hides his mediocrity behind an affectation of dignity as was dear old Yorick, of whom you will read when you have got to know the sweetness of Catullus. This Yorick it was who declared that the Frenchman's epigram describing gravity as "a mysterious carriage of the body to cover the defects of the mind," deserved "to be wrote in letters of gold"; and I make no doubt that had there been a greater recognition of the extreme value and importance of humour in the early ages of the world, our history books would record fewer blunders on the part of kings, counsellors, and princes, and the great churches would not have alienated the sympathy of so many goodly people at the most important moment in their existence—the beginning of their proselytism.

This erudite reflection is to prepare you for the introduction of my hero, Robert Stephenson Smyth Baden-Powell. I introduce him to you as a hero—and as a humourist. To me he appears the ideal English schoolboy, and the ideal British officer; but if I had blurted this out at the beginning of my story you might perhaps have flung the book into an ink-stained corner, thinking you were in for a dull lecture. It is the misfortune of goodness to be generally treated with superstitious awe, as though it were a visitant from heaven, instead of being part and parcel of our own composition. So I begin by assuring you that if ever there was a light-hearted, jovial creature it is my hero, and by promising you that he shall not bore you with moral disquisitions, nor shock your natural and untainted mind with impossible precepts.

He is a hero in the best sense of the word, living cleanly, despising viciousness equally with effeminacy, and striving after the development of his talents, just as a wise painter labours at the perfecting of his picture. Permit me here to quote the words of a sagacious Florentine gentleman named Guicciardini: "Men," says he, "are all by nature more inclined to do good than ill; nor is there anybody who, where he is not by some strong consideration pulled the other way, would not more willingly do good than ill."

Goodness, then, is a part of our being; therefore when you are behaving yourself like a true man, do not flatter yourself that you are doing any superhuman feat. And do not, as some do, have a sort of stupid contempt for people who respect truth, honesty, and purity, people who work hard at school, never insult their masters, and try to get on in the world without soiling their fingers and draggling their skirts in the mire. But see you cultivate humour as you go along. Without that there is danger in the other.

It is useful to reflect that no man without the moral idea ever wrought our country lasting service or won himself a place in the hearts of mankind. On the other hand, most of the men whose names are associated in your mind with courage and heroism are those who keenly appreciated the value of Conduct, and strove valiantly to keep themselves above the demoralising and vulgarising influences of the world.

Baden-Powell, then, is a hero, but no prodigy. He is a hero, and human. A ripple of laughter runs through his life, the fresh wind blows about him as he comes smiling before our eyes; and if he be too full of fun and good spirits to play the part of King Arthur in your imagination, be sure that no knight of old was ever more chivalrous towards women, more tender to children, and more resolved upon walking cleanly through our difficult world.

Ask those who know him best what manner of man he is, and the immediate answer, made with merry eyes and a deep chuckle, is this: "He's the funniest beggar on earth." And then when you have listened to many stories of B.-P.'s pranks, your informant will grow suddenly serious and tell you what a "straight" fellow he is, what a loyal friend, what an enthusiastic soldier. But it is ever his fun first.

One word more. Against such a work as this it is sometimes urged that there is a certain indelicacy in revealing the virtues of a living man to whomsoever has a shilling in his pocket to purchase a book. My answer to such a charge may be given in a few lines. In writing about Baden-Powell your humble servant has hardly considered the feelings of Baden-Powell at all. B.-P. has outlived a goodly number of absurd newspaper biographies, and he will survive this. Of you, and you alone, most honoured sir, has the present historian thought, and so long as you are pleased, it matters little to him if the hypersensitive lift up lean hands, turn pale eyes to Heaven, and squeak "Indecent!" till they are hoarse. And now, with as little moralising as possible, and no more cautions, let us get along with our story.

CHAPTER II

THE FAMILY

Baden-Powell had certain advantages in birth. We will not violently uproot the family tree, nor will we go trudging over the broad acres of early progenitors. I refer to the fact that his father was a clergyman. To be a parson's son is the natural beginning of an adventurous career; and, if we owe no greater debt to the Church of our fathers, there is always this argument in favour of the Establishment, that most of the men who have done something for our Empire have first opened eyes on this planet in some sleepy old rectory where roses bloom and rooks are blown about the sky.

Mr. Baden-Powell, the father of our hero, was a man of great powers. He was a renowned professor at Oxford, celebrated for his attainments in theology and in physical science. But the peace-loving man of letters died ere his boys had grown to youth, and, alas, the memory of him is blurred and indistinct in their minds. They remember a quiet, soft-voiced, tender-hearted man who was tall and of goodly frame, yet had the scholar's air, about whose knees they would cluster and hear enchanting tales, the plots of which have long since got tangled in the red tape of life. He had, what all fathers should surely have, a great love of natural history, and on his country walks would beguile his boys with talk of animals, birds, and flowers, implanting in their minds a love of the open and a study of field geology which has since stood them in excellent stead. I like to picture this learned professor, who was attacked by the narrow-minded Hebraists of his day for showing, as one obituary notice remarked, that the progress of modern scientific discovery, although necessitating modifications in many of the still prevailing ideas with which the Christian religion became encrusted in the times of ignorance and superstition, is in no way incompatible with a sincere and practical acceptance of its great and fundamental truths,—I like, I say, to picture this Oxford professor on one of his walks bending over pebbles, birds' eggs, and plants, with a troop of bright-eyed boys at his side. One begins to think of the scent of the hedgerow, the shimmering gossamer on the sweet meadows, the song of the invisible lark, the goodly savour of the rich earth, and then to the mind's eye, in the midst of it all, there springs the picture of the genial parson, tall and spare, surrounded by his olive-branches, and perhaps with our hero, as one of the late shoots, riding triumphant on his shoulder. It was his habit, too, when composing profound papers to read before the Royal Society, to let his children amuse themselves in his book-lined study, and who cannot see the beaming face turned often from the written sheets to look lovingly on his happy children? But, as I say, the memory of this lovable man is blurred for his children, and the clearest of their early memories are associated with their mother, into whose hands their training came while our hero was still in frocks.

Mrs. Baden-Powell's maiden name was Henrietta Grace Smyth. Her father was a sturdy seaman, Admiral W.H. Smyth, K.S.F., and fortunately for her children she was trained in a school where neither Murdstone rigour nor sentimental coddling was regarded as an essential. She was the kind of mother that rears brave men and true. For discipline she relied solely on her children's sense of honour, and for the maintenance of her influence on their character she was content to trust to a never-wavering interest in all their sports, occupations, and hobbies. Her children were encouraged to bear pain manfully, but they were not taught to crush their finer feelings. A simple form of religion was inculcated, while the boys' natural love for humour was encouraged and developed. In a word, the children were allowed to grow up naturally, and the influence brought to bear upon them by this wise mother was as quiet and as imperceptible as Nature intended it to be. Dean Stanley, Ruskin, Jowett, Tyndall, and Browning were among those who were wont to come and ply Mrs. Baden-Powell with questions as to how she managed to keep in such excellent control half-a-dozen boys filled to the brim with animal spirits. The truth is, the boys were unconscious of any controlling influence in their lives, and how could they have anything but a huge respect for a mother whose knowledge of science and natural history enabled her to tell them things which they did not know? In those days mothers were not content to commit the formation of their children's minds to nursemaids and governesses.

The eldest boy became a Chief Judge in India, and lived to write what the *Times* described as "three monumental volumes on the Land Systems of British India." The second boy, Warington, of whom we shall have more to say in the next chapter, went into the Navy, but left that gallant Service to practise at the Bar, and now is as breezy a Q.C. as ever brought the smack of salt-water into the Admiralty Court. The third son, Sir George Baden-Powell, sometime member of Parliament for Liverpool, had already entered upon a distinguished career when, to the regret of all who had marked his untiring devotion to Imperial affairs, his early death robbed the country of a loyal son. The other brothers of our hero are Frank Baden-Powell, who took Honours at Balliol, and is a barrister of the Inner Temple, as well as a noted painter, and Baden F.S. Baden-Powell, Major in the Scots Guards, whose war-kites at Modder River enabled Marconi's staff to establish wireless telegraphy across a hundred miles of South Africa. Among this family of young lions there was one little girl, Agnes, as keen about natural history as the rest, to whom her brothers were as earnestly and as passionately devoted as ever was Don Quixote to his Dulcinea.

And now to little Robert Stephenson Smyth Baden-Powell in knickerbockers and Holland jerkin.

CHAPTER III

HOME LIFE AND HOLIDAYS

Baden-Powell is now called either "B.-P." or "Bathing Towel." To his family he has always been Ste. This name, a contraction of Stephenson, was found for him by his big brothers in the days when home-made soldiers and birds'-nesting were life's main business.

Ste, who we must record was born at 6 Stanhope Street, London, on the 22nd February 1857, and had the engineer Robert Stephenson for one of his godfathers, was educated at home until he was eleven years of age. His parents had a great dread of overtaxing young brains, and lessons were never made irksome to any of their children. Ste learned to straddle a pony very soon after he had mastered the difficult business of walking, and with long hours spent in the open in the lively companionship of his brothers he grew up in vigorous and healthy boyhood. He had an enquiring mind, and never seemed to look upon lessons as a "fag." He was always "wanting to know," and there was almost as much eagerness on the little chap's part to be able to decline *mensa* and conjugate *amo* as he evinced in competing with his brothers in their sports and games. Such was his gentle, placid nature that the tutor who looked after his work loved to talk with people about his charge, never tiring in reciting little instances of the boy's delicacy of feeling and his intense eagerness to learn. Mark well, Smith minor, that this is no little Paul Dombey of whom you are reading. B.-P., so far as I can discover, never heard in the tumbling of foam-crested waves on the level sands of the sea-shore any mysterious message to his individual soul from the spirit world. He was full of fun, full of the joy of life, and as "keen as mustard" on adventures of any kind. His fun, however, was of the innocent order. He was not like Cruel Frederick in *Struwwelpeter*, who (the little beast!) delighted in tearing the wings from flies and hurling brickbats at starving cats. Baden-Powell would have kicked Master Frederick rather severely if he had caught him at any such mean business. No, his fun took quite another form. He was fond of what you call "playing the fool," singing comic songs, learning to play tunes on every odd musical instrument he could find, and delighting his brothers by "taking off" people of their acquaintance. B.-P., you must know, is a first-rate actor, and in his boyhood it was one of his chief delights to write plays for himself and his brothers to act. Some of these plays were moderately clever, but all of them contained a screamingly funny part for the low comedian of the company—our friend Ste himself.

Another of his amusements at this time was sketching. He got into the habit of holding his pencil or paint-brush in the left hand, and his watchful mother was troubled in her mind as to the wisdom of allowing a possible Botticelli to play pranks with his art. One day Ruskin called when this doubt was in her mind, and to him the question was propounded. Without a moment's reflection he counselled the mother to let the boy draw in whatsoever manner he listed, and together they went to find the young artist at his work. In the play-room they discovered one brother reading hard at astronomy, and Ste with a penny box of water-colours painting for dear life—with his left hand.

"Now I'll show you how to paint a picture," said Ruskin, and with a piece of paper on the top of his hat and B.-P.'s penny box of paints at his side he set to work, taking a little china vase for a model. Both the vase and the picture are now in the drawing-room of Mrs. Baden-Powell's London house. The result of Ruskin's advice was that B.-P. continued to draw with his left hand, and now in making sketches he finds no difficulty in drawing with his left hand and shading in at the same time with his right.

There is an incident of his childhood which I must not forget to record. At a dinner-party at the Baden-Powells', when Ste was not yet three years old, the guests being all learned and distinguished men, such as Buckle and Whewell, Thackeray was handing Mrs. Baden-Powell into dinner when he noticed that one of the little children was following behind. This was the future scout of the British Army, and the young gentleman, according to his wont, was just scrambling into a chair when Thackeray, fumbling in his pocket, produced a new shilling, and said in his caressing voice, "There, little one, you shall have this shilling if you are good and run away." Ste quietly looked up at his mother, and not until she told him that he might go up to the nursery did he shift his ground. But he carried that shilling with him, and now it is one of his most treasured possessions.

While he was doing lessons at home Baden-Powell gave evidence of his bent. He was fond of geography, and few things pleased him more than the order to draw a map. His maps, by the way, were always drawn with his left hand, and were astonishingly neat and accurate. Then in his spare hours, with scissors and paper, he would cut out striking resemblances of the most noted animals in the Zoo, and these—elephants and tigers, monkeys and bears—were "hung" by his admiring brothers with due honour on a large looking-glass in the schoolroom, there to amuse the juvenile friends of the family. He had the knack, too, of closely imitating the various sounds made by animals and birds, and one of his infant jokes was to steal behind a person's chair and suddenly break forth "with conspuent doodle-doo." And, again, when he was a little older, living at Rosenheim, I.W., there was surely the future defender of Mafeking in the little chap in brown Holland on the sands of Bonchurch digging scientific trenches with wooden spade, and demonstrating to his governess the impregnability of his sand fortress. With his sister and brother, little Ste was once out with this governess on a country ramble near Tunbridge

Wells, when the governess discovered that she had walked farther than she intended and was in strange country. Ste was elated. But enquiry elicited the information that the party was not lost, and that they could return home by a shorter route; then was Baden-Powell miserable and cast down. He protested that he wanted the party to get lost so that he could find the way home for them.

A favourite holiday haunt was Tunbridge Wells, where Ste's grandfather owned a spacious and a fair demesne. Here, with miles of wood for exploration, brothers and sister were in their element. They would climb into the highest chestnut trees in the woods, taking up hampers and hay for the construction of nests, and at that exalted altitude play all manner of wild and romantic games. And yet they would also take up books into those cool branches and do lessons! Of Ste at this period his governess remarks, "It gave him great pleasure to enter a new rule in arithmetic"—an illuminative sentence, in which one sees the governess as well as the child.

It was here in Tunbridge Wells that Ste, with little Baden, now Guardsman and inventor of war-kites, spent laborious days in constructing a really serviceable dam in the river, digging there a deep hole in order to make themselves a luxurious bathing-place. From early infancy they had been taught to do for themselves. Master B.-P. could dress and undress himself before he was three years old, and at three he could speak tolerably well in German as well as English. The children were encouraged to get knowledge as some other children are encouraged to get bumptiousness; their parents delighted, and showed the children their delight, whenever a child did something sensible and clever; there was no unintelligent admiration of precocity.

The boys dug their own gardens, and from five years of age each child kept a most careful book of his expenditure by double entry. Their pennies went chiefly in books and presents, and omnibuses for long excursions out of London. There was no prohibition as to sweets, but never a penny of these earnest young double-entry bookkeepers found its way to the tuck-shop. However, a joke among the brothers was the following constant entry in the book of one of them: "Orange, L0:0:1." But no chaff was strong enough to correct that healthy appetite, and "Orange, L0:0:1" went on through the happy years.

At eleven years of age, Ste was packed off to a small private school, and here he distinguished himself in the same manner, though of course on a smaller scale, as Mr. Gladstone did at Eton. His moral courage, coupled with his athletic prowess, made him the darling of the little school, and the headmaster sorrowfully told his mother when the boy's two years' schooling were over that he would thankfully keep him there without fee of any kind, because by force of character the plucky little fellow had raised the entire moral tone of the school.

And now we come to what I regard as the most important part of our hero's life. In the last chapter I said we should have to say something about B.-P.'s big brother, the sailor, Warington, named after his grandmother, who was a Warington of Waddon Park. The very name Warington, even though it be spelled with a single 'r,' has an inspiring sound, and while Thackeray lives will ever be linked with all that is true and straightforward in the human heart. Imagine the reverence felt for Warington by the young brothers when he came home from a sea voyage! Not only were there the broad square shoulders, the deep chest, and the bronzed face to compel admiration; but a masterful and commanding manner withal, a stern eye and a rousing voice—and the overwhelming and crushing fact that he was a British Naval officer! Warington had been born ten years before Ste, and it is a mighty good thing for B.-P. (and he would be the first to admit it) that this was the case. For I believe that the resourcefulness of Baden-Powell is the result of the early training which he received at the hands of Warington; without that training he would have grown up a delightful and an amusing fellow, but, I suspect, as so many delightful and amusing people are, ineffective. And that is just what B.-P. is not.

You must know that in the spring holidays the boys spent their days in ranging field and copse "collecting," riding ponies, often with their faces towards the tail-end, attending to their innumerable pets, and doing a certain amount of reading of their own free will. Ste's study was mainly history and geology, and it was his custom to embellish the pages of the books he was reading with suitable illustrations as he went along. With these amusements, and always a good many productions of Ste's original comedies, the spring holidays slipped away pleasantly enough. But in the summer holidays came Warington fresh from the sea, with abounding energy and indomitable will, and recreation then was of a sterner kind.

Warington had designed a yacht, a smart 5-tonner, and in supreme command of this little craft, with his brothers for the crew, and only one hired hand for the dirty work, he took the schoolboys away from the ease and comforts of home life to rough it at sea. They shipped as seamen, and as seamen they lived. It was a case of "lights out" soon after dusk, and then up again with the sun. This rule, however, was not followed with comfortable regularity, for sometimes stress of weather would find the little chaps tumbling out of their hammocks in the dead of night, and clambering upon deck with knuckles rubbing the sleep out of their eyes. All the work usually performed by seamen, with the sole exception of cooking, was done by these little chaps, and under the eagle eye of Warington it was well and truly done. Not that they showed any disposition to shirk. On the contrary, a keener crew was never shipped, but there was something in their knowledge that the skipper's word was law, that there was no arguing about orders, which must have given a certain polish to their work. Warington, of course, was no petty tyrant, lording it over young brothers, and swaggering in the undisputed character of his sway. Like the rest he is a humourist, and when a gale was not blowing or the yacht was not contesting a race, he was as full of merriment and good spirits as the rest. His opinion of Ste at this time was a high one. He was always, says he, "most dependable." Receiving his orders, the future defender of Mafeking would stand as stiff and silent as a rock, showing scarce a sign that he understood them, but the orders were always carried out to the letter, and in a thoroughly finished and seamanlike manner. Ste was always the tallest of his brothers, and at this time he was singularly lithe and wiry. A tall slight boy with quite fair hair, a brown skin, and sharp brown eyes, he possessed extraordinary powers of endurance, and could always outlast the rest of the brothers. He was quick to perceive the reason of an order, and always quick to carry it out; he was just as brisk in organising cruises on his own account, when, with the leave of Skipper Warington, he would take command of the yacht's dinghy and go off on fishing expeditions with Baden and Frank. It was a dinghy that moved quickly with a sail, but in all their cruises up creeks and round about the hulks of Portsmouth Harbour they never came to grief, and always returned with a good catch of bass and mullet.

Danger did come to the yacht itself, however, on more than one occasion, and but for the courage and skill of Warington, the world might never have heard of B.-P. and the other brothers. Once, in the *Koh-i-noor* (a 10-tonner with about eighteen tons displacement), which was the second yacht designed by Warington, the boys were cruising about the south coast, when, towards evening, just off Torquay, a gale got up, and the sea began to get uncommon rough. As the gale increased almost to a hurricane and the waves dashed a larger amount of spray over the gunwale of the gallant little yacht, Warington decided to change his course and run back to Weymouth. The night was getting dark, and the storm increased. To add to the anxieties of the skipper his crew of boys, though showing no funk, began to grow green about the gills, and presently Warington found himself in command of an entirely sea-sick crew. He was unable to leave the helm, and for over thirty-one hours he stood there, giving his orders in a cheerful voice to the groaning youngsters who were more than once driven to the ship's drenched and dripping side. Fortunately Warington knew the coast well, for it was much too dark to see a chart, and so, despite the raging tempest, the 10-tonner fought her way through the waves while the sea broke continually over her side, drenching the shivering boys, who stuck to their posts, and every now and then shouted to each other with chattering teeth that it was "awful fun."

As showing the resourcefulness of the crew, I may narrate another yachting story. One Saturday, off Yarmouth, when the Baden-Powells were thinking of a race for which they were entered on the following Monday, a storm suddenly came on, which played such havoc with the rigging that the mast was snapped in two, and the whole racing kit went overboard. With clenched teeth the youngsters set to work and, with many a long pull and a strong pull, got all the wreck on board. Then with axes they slashed away at the wire-rigging, and set to work to rig up a jury-mast. All Sunday they toiled—the spars on an 18-tonner are no child's play—and at last they were able to rig up a jury-mast which would carry the mainsail with four reefs, while the foresail was able to catch the wind of heaven with only two. On Monday morning the yacht sailed out of Yarmouth fully rigged, and made off to the regatta with as cheerful a crew as ever braved the elements. The result of this labour was that the Baden-Powells, with a jury rig, won a second prize, and came in for the warm commendation of wondering and admiring sailors.

As I have said, in these expeditions the boys did seamen's work. They learned how to set sails, how to splice, how to reeve gear, how to moor a ship, and make all ready for scrubbing the bottom. It was a fine sight to see the healthy younkers, with trousers rolled over the knee, ankles well under slate-coloured oozing mud, scrubbing away at the bottom of the ship, and laughing and singing among themselves, while the reflective Warington, pipe in mouth, looked on and encouraged the toilers.

All round the English coast sailed the Baden-Powells, fighting their way to glory in regattas, and enjoying themselves from sunrise to sunset. On racing days it was a case of "strictly to business," and each boy had his proper station and knew well how to pull or slack out ropes. On other days it was a case of fun and frolic, and here, of course, B.-P. was the life and soul of the party. There were no squabbles, no petty jealousies; never did the brothers throughout their boyhood come to fisticuffs. But while there was perfect equality among them and no favouritism was ever shown, Ste was regarded as the prime comedian, and there was never any question that when theatricals were the order of the day he should reign in supreme command.

One of the houses taken by Mrs. Baden-Powell for the holidays was Llandogo Falls, a most romantic place on the Wye, the property of Mr. Gallenga, the Italian correspondent of the *Times*, who had previously got mixed up in a deep political plot in Italy, whereby he gained many useful secrets, but whereby, at the same time, he was obliged to flee out of Italy and return to England. We fancy this story in its full details must have appealed strongly to the imagination of Baden-Powell, whose after-life, could it be fully written, would satisfy the keenest appetite for daring, excitement, and romance. But to return to Llandogo Falls. Mrs. Baden-Powell, her daughter, and all the servants made the journey from London by means of the railway; but to the boys the fastest of express trains would have seemed slow, and accordingly Warington made ready his collapsible boat, and, rowing by day and sleeping on board by night, these indefatigable youngsters left London behind them, crossed the Severn, and, pulling up the Wye, arrived at Llandogo Falls, the first intimation of their arrival to Mrs. Baden-Powell being the sight of them dragging the boat over the lawn to the stables. This feat succeeded in endearing them to the Welsh people in the neighbourhood, who were greatly struck by the courage of the boys in crossing the Severn in a collapsible boat.

Here, at Llandogo Falls, the boys spent a great deal of time in riding practically wild ponies, and even in those days Ste was famous for his graceful seat, his quiet patience with an untract-able steed, and his daring in attempting difficult jumps.

Besides riding, the boys were fond of wandering about the country, making friends with the natives, shooting birds to be presently stuffed by themselves and put in the family museum, collecting rare insects, examining old ruins, and rowing up the Wye to spend the afternoon in bathing or in fishing, sometimes in both.

In this simple, healthy, and thoroughly English fashion the Baden-Powells spent their holidays, and in their home-life grew up devoted to each other, and to the mother whose controlling influence was over all their sports and occupations. It is interesting to note, ere we leave the subject of early training, that no infliction of punishment in any shape or form was permitted by Mrs. Baden-Powell. Whether such a rule would work for good in all families is a question that I for one, as a father of a young family, will never imperil my reputation for consistency by answering with a dogmatic affirmative. Nevertheless, one recognises the truth of Nietzsche's warning, "Beware of him in whom the impulse to punish is powerful." In the case of the Baden-Powells the proof of the pudding is in the eating, and you will get none of them to say that their childhood was not a joyous period, while Mrs. Baden-Powell will contend with any mother under Heaven that never before were such honourable, straightforward, and gentle-minded children. This home-life has never lost its charm, and though the sons may be scattered over the world on the Queen's service, they come back to exchange memories with each other under their mother's roof as often as the exigencies of their professions will allow. And when B.-P. is in the house, though his hair begins to flourish less willingly on his brow, he is just like the boy of old, springing up the stairs three steps at a time, and whistling as he goes with a heartiness and a joyousness that astonishes the decorous ten-year-old sparrow Timothy as he flits about the house after Miss Baden-Powell.

I have in my possession a copy of Mr. Russell's monograph on Mr. Gladstone, which had fallen into the hands of a grand old Tory parson. The margins of those pages bristle with the vehement annotations of my old friend. Against the statement that Mr. Gladstone had "a nature completely unspoilt by success and prominence and praise," there is a vigorous "OH!" Where it is recorded how in 1874 Mr. Gladstone promised to repeal the income-tax, I find a pencil line and the contemptuous comment, "A bribe for power!" Mr. Forster's resignation of office in 1882 is hailed with a joyful "Bravo, Forster!" and so on throughout Mr. Russell's interesting book. But on the last page of all there are three pencil lines marking a sentence, and by the side of the lines the concession, "Yes— true." The sentence is this: "But the noblest natures are those which are seen at their best in the close communion of the home."

CHAPTER IV

CARTHUSIAN

A gentleman once wrote to the late headmaster of Charterhouse, Dr. William Haig-Brown, saying that he wished to have his son "interred" at that school. The headmaster wrote back immediately saying he would be glad to "undertake" the boy. The same headmaster being shown over a model farm remarked of the ornamental piggery, built after the manner of a Chinese Pagoda, that if there was Pagoda outside there was certainly pig odour inside.

Such a man as this is sure to have been impressed by the personality of Master Ste, who, in 1870, came to him in the old Charterhouse, that hoary, venerable pile which seems to shrink into itself, as if to shut out the unpoetic and modern atmosphere of Smithfield Meat Market. B.-P. went to Charterhouse as a gown boy, nominated by the Duke of Marlborough, and owing to the ease with which his infant studies had been conducted, was obliged to enter by a low form. But he had, as we have already said, an enquiring mind. He had also a clear brain, all the better for not having been crammed in childhood; and, therefore, strong in body, full of health and good spirits, and just as keen to get knowledge as to get a rare bird's egg, he began his school-days with everything in his favour. The result was that 1874 found him in the sixth, and one of the brilliant boys of his time.

Dr. Haig-Brown, as we have said, was sure to have been

Harold Begbie

impressed by B.-P., and there is no need for his assurance that he remembers the boy perfectly. Of course, when one sits in his medieval study and asks the Doctor to discourse of B.-P., he begins by recalling Ste's love of fun; indeed, it is with no great willingness that he leaves that view of his pupil. But the boy's inflexibility of purpose, his uprightness and his eagerness to learn are as equally impressed upon the headmaster's mind, and he likes to talk about the exhilarating effect which B.-P.'s virile character had upon the moral tone of the school. "I never doubted his word," Dr. Haig-Brown told me, and by the tone of the headmaster's voice one realised that B.-P. was just one of those boys whose word it is impossible to doubt. A clean, self-respecting boy.

He was the life of the school in those entertainments for which Charterhouse has always been famous, and his reputation as a wit followed him from the stage into the playground. B.-P. was a keen footballer, and whenever he kept goal there was always a knot of grinning boys round the posts listening with huge delight to their hero's facetiae. He also had the habit, such were his animal spirits, of giving the most nerve-fluttering war-whoop imaginable when rushing the ball forward, and this cry is said to have been of so terrifying a nature as to fling the opposing side into a state of fear not very far removed from absolute panic. By the way, it is interesting in the light of after-events to read in the school's *Football Annual* (1876, p. 30) that "R.S.S. B.-P. is a good goalkeeper, *keeping cool, and always to be depended upon.*"

But it was not only at football that Baden-Powell spent his time in the playground, although it was only in football that he shone. Into every game he threw himself with zest and earnestness, playing hard for his side, and finding himself always regarded by his opponents as an enemy to be treated with respect. That he continued to play cricket, racquets, and fives, although not a great success, is characteristic of his devotion to sports, and his habit of doing what is the right thing to do. Then he was a faithful and lively contributor to the school magazine, added his lusty young voice to the chapel choir, and was for ever seeking out excuses for getting up theatricals. Of one of his performances at the end of the Long Quarter in 1872 it is interesting to note that the *Era* of that time remarked that it was "full of vivacity and mischief." He was always a great success as an old woman, and we shall see that in later days he played a woman's part with huge success in far Afghanistan. At one of these school entertainments big brother Warington was present, and he laughingly recalls how the vast audience of shiny-faced boys broke into a great roar of delight directly B.-P. appeared in the wings—before he had uttered a word or made a grimace. Dr. Haig-Brown and the other masters who remember B.-P. like to recall scenes of this kind, and it is no disparagement of Ste's other sterling qualities that they seem to have been more impressed by his excellent fooling than by any other of his good qualities. It is the greater tribute to his genius for acting.

So long as the world lasts, I suppose, the intelligent boy who works hard at school will play the clown's part in popular fiction. Tom Sawyer is the kind of youth we like to see given the chief part in a novel, while George Washington, we are all agreed, is fit target for our lofty scorn. But how few of the people we love to read about in the airy realm of fiction, or the still airier realm of history, really possess our hearts? Think over the heroes in novels who would be drawn in with both hands to the fireside did they step out from between covers and present themselves at our front door in flesh as solid as the oak itself. And the good boy in fiction is anathema. Shakespeare himself believed that

Love goes towards love, as schoolboys from their books;

and the man is regarded almost as un-English who would have the world believe that there are British boys for whom the acquisition of knowledge has almost the same attraction as for their heroes in fiction has the acquisition of somebody's apples, or the tormenting of helpless animals.

The fault is not with the world but with the silly writers of goody-goody stories, who have so emasculated and effeminated the boy who works hard and holds his head high that it is now well-nigh impossible to hear of such an one in real life without instantly setting him down as an intolerable prig. These writers have committed the greatest crime against their creations that authors can commit—they have made them non-human. If the stories about George Washington had narrated how on one occasion he laughed uproariously, or how he once ate too many mince-pies, he might have escaped the lamentable and unjust reputation which seems likely to be his fate for another aeon or two. That boys can be good and human everybody knows, and the man who loves Tom Sawyer and sneers at Eric would be the first to flog and abuse his son if he bore a closer resemblance to the former than to the latter.

Baden-Powell as a boy was delightful. A grin always hovered about his face, and the Spirit of Fun herself looked out of his sharp, brown eyes. He was for ever making "the other chaps" roar; keeping a football field on the giggle; sending a concert-audience into fits. But he was just the sort of schoolboy of whom there would be no incidents to record. Men who knew him and lived with him in those days remember him, perhaps, more distinctly than any other boy of their time, and at the merest mention of his name their eyes twinkle with delight. "Oh, old Bathing Towel. George! what a funny beggar he was. Remember him? I should think I did. Stories about him? Well, I don't remember any just now, but dear old Bathing Towel—!" and off they go into another roar of laughter. All they can tell you is how he used to act and recite, and play all manner of musical instruments, or, if you drag them away from the stage, how he used to rend the air with his terrible war-whoop at the critical moment in a football match.

But although this is how it strikes a contemporary, Baden-Powell was in deadly earnest when it was a matter of books and ink-pots. He might be the funny man of the school, but he was also one of the most brilliant. He gave his masters the impression of a boy who really delighted in getting on; who was really keen about mastering a difficult subject. His vivacity and freshness, his energy and vigour, helped him to take pleasure in work which to another boy, less physically blessed, would have been an irksome toil; but though his body may have projected him some distance upon his way, it was his soul that really carried him triumphantly through. The spirit of Baden-Powell in those days was what it is now—supremely intent upon beating down obstacles in his path, and resolute to do well whatever the moment's duty might be. So the boy who was setting a football field on the roar at one moment, at the next would be sitting with fixed eyes and knit brows, "hashing" at Latin verses, as serious as a leader-writer hurling his bolts at the European Powers.

The master who best remembers B.-P. is Mr. Girdlestone, in whose house our hero spent four years of his school-days. Looking back over the past Mr. Girdlestone finds that what impressed him most in B.-P. during his school-days was the boy's manner with his elders. He was reserved, very reserved, and he never had any one close chum at school; but apparently he was quite free of shyness, as he would approach his masters without any trace of that timidity which too often marks the commerce of boy with master. On an afternoon's walk, for instance, B.-P. would not be found among the boys, but side by side deep in conversation with his master. And these conversations, I find, convinced his gubernators that he was very much above the average cut of boy in intelligence; not (Heaven forbid!) that he made parade of his little knowledge, but rather that he was eager to get information in really useful subjects from his superiors, and not above boldly declaring his eagerness. In those days Dr. Haig-Brown had a great reputation for sternness, and it is said that even the masters would sometimes quail when they entered his presence; but B.-P. was perfectly at his ease and entirely self-possessed even in approaching the presence of the great Doctor. He was never bashful in addressing a master on new schemes for the benefit of the school, and it was solely owing to his application to Mr. Girdlestone that Charterhouse first started its string orchestra, which is now one of the best boys' bands in the kingdom. Music, it seems, was one of his chief delights at school, he played the violin really well; but while he loved that king of instruments, he would stoop to baser, and oft delight his contemporaries, holding them entranced, by spirited performances on the mouth organ and the ocarina.

With no close friend Baden-Powell was a boy without an enemy, and his popularity may be seen in many ways. Although, for instance, he was not successful in athletics, he was a regular member of the Sports Committee, and worked with intense enthusiasm for the success of Sports-Day. And, another instance; as a memento of their favourite, the butler of B.-P.'s house and his wife saved a part of the dress he wore in his last theatrical performance. When the news came of the relief of Ladysmith this garment was drawn forth from the back of a drawer and used as a flag of rejoicing, and as I write it is being jealously guarded to be hung out from the school windows when the little boy who wore it is delivered from his glorious prison of Mafeking.

This butler has a very vivid recollection of Baden-Powell. He remembers him as a boy "up to mischief," but too much of a gentleman ever to go beyond proper bounds. His mischief was of the harmless nature, and he was never "shown up" for a row of any description. Many a time did the observant butler come upon Baden-Powell in the House Music Room practising his tunes; but not by any means in a dull and unoriginal fashion. It was the boy's habit to take off his boots and stockings, set a chair on a table, climb up to his perch, and from thence draw forth melody of sorts with his ten toes. After this it is surely a wonder that Baden-Powell in joining the army did not insist upon doing Manual Exercise with his extremities.

There is a story about Master Ste which clearly shows, I think, the estimation in which he was held by the other boys. Who but a general favourite could have played the following part? On Shrove Tuesday at Charterhouse there was of old time a custom called the Lemon Peel Fight. With every pancake the boys were given a lemon, or half a lemon, and these were never eaten, being jealously reserved for the great fight on the green outside after the pancakes had unmysteriously disappeared. On one occasion, when the sides were drawn up in grim battle array, facing each other lemon in hand, every boy as dauntless as Horatius, Herminius, and Spurius Lartius, and just when the signal for the conflict was to be given,—suddenly upon the scene appeared Baden-Powell, swathed from head to foot in tremendous padding, with nothing to be seen of his little brown face save the bright, mischievous eyes peeping out of two slits. Rushing between the two lines with a fearsome war-whoop, this alarming apparition squatted suddenly upon the grass, and looking first on one army and then on the other, said in the most nonchalant tone of voice: "Let the battle commence!"

From the battle-field one goes naturally to the butts. In some of the newspaper articles concerning Baden-Powell it has been said that he had nothing to do with the Rifle Corps. This is quite wrong. There was nothing going on at Charterhouse into which Baden-Powell did not fling himself with infinite zest, and shooting, of course, had special attractions for a boy bred in the country and deep-learned in the mysteries of field and covert. Not only did he take part in the shooting, but he was an active member of the Shooting Committee. His last score, shooting as a member of the School VIII. *versus* the 6th Regiment at Aldershot on 6th March 1876, was as follows:—

200 yards	500 yards	Total
22	14	36

The school was beaten, and Sergeant B.-P. came out of the contest as third best shot for Charterhouse. The day, says the historian, was bitterly cold, and a violent and gusty wind blew across the range. Seven shots were fired at each distance, class targets being used.

If there is interest in Baden-Powell's score as a schoolboy-marksman, how much greater interest should there be in Baden-Powell's hit as orator? It is not always the ready actor who makes the best polemical speech, but Baden-Powell had a reputation at Charterhouse as a debater as well as fame as a mimic. That the boy was more than ordinarily intelligent may even be seen in the abbreviated report of one of his speeches preserved in the school magazine. The subject of debate was that "Marshal Bazaine was a traitor to his country," and Baden-Powell spoke against the motion. The report says that he "appeared to be firmly convinced that the French plan of the war was to get the Prussians between Sedan and Metz, and play a kind of game of ball with them. By surrendering, Bazaine saved lives which would be of use against the Communists. As there was only a government *de facto* in Paris he was compelled to act for himself." But even eloquence of this order was not sufficient to persuade Charterhouse that Bazaine deserved no censure. The motion was carried by a majority of 1.

In those days, too, Baden-Powell was famous as an artist, and his sketches, with the left hand, were admired and commented upon by masters as well as boys. One can fancy with what great reverence B.-P. the caricaturist must have looked upon Thackeray's pencil in the Charterhouse Library—the pencil of the great man whose shilling he was then hoarding with the jealousy of a miser.

Baden-Powell's quality as a schoolboy may be judged by his later life. Few things are so pleasant about him as his intense loyalty to his old school. Before leaving India for England in 1898, he wrote to Mr. Girdlestone, asking his old House Master to send to his London address a list of all the interesting fixtures at Charterhouse, so that he might see what was going on directly he arrived in England. Whenever he is in the old country he pays a visit to Godalming, and one of his last acts before leaving for South Africa was to call on Dr. Haig-Brown at the Charterhouse, where he first went to school, to bid his old Head a brave and cheerful farewell. And what was more English, what more typical of the public-school man, than the letter B.-P. sent to England from bombarded Mafeking, saying that he had been looking up old Carthusians to join him in a dinner on Founder's Day? In India he never allowed the 12th of December to pass unhonoured, and whether he be journeying through the bush of the Gold Coast Hinterland, or riding across the South African veldt, he is always quick to recognise the face of an old schoolboy, or the Carthusian colours in a necktie.

The estimation in which Charterhouse holds Baden-Powell may be seen in the result of a "whip round" for the hero besieged in Mafeking—nearly a hundred and forty cases of useful goods. These cases contained, among other things, 962 lbs. of tobacco, 1200 cigars, 23,000 cigarettes, 640 pipes, 160 dozens of wine and spirits, seven cases of provisions, 490 shirts, 730 "helmets," 1350 pairs of socks, and 168 pairs of boots. In addition to this over L1000 was raised by Old Carthusians to be sent out in its own useful shape.

Popularity such as this has been justly earned. Baden-Powell's record as a Carthusian will, as we have seen, bear looking into, and though the old school may boast of more brilliant scholars and more world-wide names on its roll, I do not think it has ever sent into the world a more useful all-round man, a more intrepid soldier, a more upright gentleman, and a more loyal son. And one knows that there is no British cheer so likely to touch the heart of Baden-Powell when he returns to England as the great roar which will assuredly go up in Charterhouse when this Old Boy comes beaming into the Great Hall.

Harold Begbie

CHAPTER V

THE DASHING HUSSAR

When Baden-Powell turned his back on Charterhouse it was with the intention of proceeding to Oxford. Professor Jowett, who, by the bye, was the godfather of Baden, begged our hero to pay him a visit as soon as he left school, and when on this visit the Master heard that B.-P. could only spare two years for Oxford, he said, "Then Christ Church is the college for you, because at Balliol I like each man to remain three or four years, and go in for honours finally." So Ste made plans for going to Christ Church, was examined, accepted for the following term, and Dean Liddell arranged about rooms for him in the House. But ere B.-P. went up, an Army examination came on, and, "just for fun," up went our indefatigable hero with a light heart and no other thought in his mind than the determination to do his level best. The result of this happy-go-lucky entrance for examination was the unlooked-for success of our "unbruised youth with unstuffed brain," who passed second out of seven hundred and eighteen candidates, among whom, by the way, were twenty-eight University candidates. As a reward for his brilliancy, B.-P. was informed by the Duke of Cambridge that his commission would be ante-dated two years.

Until this memorable event Baden-Powell had expressed no special predilection for soldiering. His chief desire had been to go in for some profession that would take him abroad and show him the world. The first service which seemed to attract him definitely at all was the Indian Woods and Forests, and this chiefly on account of a burning desire to roam about the gorgeous East. It was only when an elder brother suggested that, if he wanted to see India and other countries as well, he might be better suited in the Army, that this born soldier gave any indication of his desire for a military career. And only with the Army examination successfully conquered did he seriously begin to think of uniforms and swords and the glamour of a soldier's life.

On the 11th September 1876 Baden-Powell joined the 13th Hussars in India, and one of his first acts was to take from his baggage an ocarina, and having assembled all the European children he could find in the station, to march at their head through the streets of Lucknow, playing with great feeling, which suffered, however, a little from his all-comprehensive grin, "The Girl I Left Behind Me." In this manner he signalised his arrival, earning the undying love of every English mother in the place, and infusing into the gallant 13th Hussars (*Viret in AEternum!*) fresh vigour and fresh spirit.

The 13th Hussars, Sir Baker Russell's old regiment, boasts a fine record, and the songs in the canteen at night will tell you how the regiment rode on the right of the line at Balaclava, when it was known to fame as the 13th Light Dragoons. One of these songs begins:—

> Six hundred stalwart warriors, of England's pride the best,
> Did grasp the lance and sabre on Balaclava's crest,
> And with their trusty leader, Lord Cardigan the brave,
> Charged up to spike the Russian guns—or find a soldier's grave.

And the refrain, which every man present sings with a face as solemn as my Lord Chancellor sitting on the Woolsack half an hour longer than usual, runs in this fashion:—

> Oh, 'tis a famous story; proclaim it far and wide,
> And let your children's children re-echo it with pride,
> How Cardigan the fearless his name immortal made,

When he crossed the Russian valley with his famous Light
Brigade.

This is the great glory of the regiment, the knowledge of which
makes the recruit blow his chest out another inch and straightway purchase out of his pay spurs that jingle more musically
when he goes abroad than the miserable things served out by
an unromantic Government. Other legends there are in this
regiment, and once Baden-Powell and his great friend, Captain
MacLaren (known to the officers as "The Boy," to the men as
"The Little Prince"), set about compiling its history; but for
some reason or another that work has not yet appeared, and
since its inception B.-P. has deserted to the Dragoons—
Vestigia nulla retrorsum!

Baden-Powell became popular with his brother-officers directly
he joined. It was his freshness, his overflowing good spirits, his
hearty and unmistakable enjoyment of life, that first won their
regard. The boy suddenly dropped into their midst was no
blase youth, no mere swaggering puppy. He was afire with the
joy of existence, radiant with happiness, excited—and not
ashamed to show it—by all the newness and fascination of
Indian life. The Major screwed his eye-glass into his eye and
smiled encouragingly; the Adjutant measured him with peg to
his lip and knew he would do. Every one felt that the new sub
was an acquisition.

But it must not be supposed that there was any "bounce"
about the new boy. Apart from his breeding and training,
which would effectually prevent a man from committing the
unpardonable sin of the social world, Baden-Powell by nature
was, and still is, a little bashful. There are people who pooh-
pooh the very idea of such a thing, and declare that the man
they have heard act and sing and play the fool is no more
nervous than a bishop among curates. Nevertheless they are
wrong; and your humble servant entirely right. B.-P., like the
other members of his family, suffers from nervousness, and
when he goes on the stage to act, and sits down at the piano to
"vamp," it is a sheer triumph of will over nerves. He is not

nervous under the wide and starry sky, not bashful when he pricks his horse into the long grass of the veldt and bears down upon a bunch of bloodthirsty savages, not nervous when he gets a child on his knee all by himself and tells her delightful stories,—but nervous as a boy on his first day at school when he finds himself being lionised in a drawing-room, or picked out of the ruck of guests for any particular notice. And so when he joined the 13th, behind the ebullient spirits was this innate bashfulness, which, added to the natural modesty of a gentleman, kept his animal spirits in a delightful simmer, and found favour for him in the eyes of his superior officers. How they discovered B.-P.'s quality as a humourist happened in this way. A day or two after he joined there was an entertainment of some sort going on in barracks, and during a pause Sir Baker Russell turned round to Baden-Powell, and said, "Here, young 'un, you can play a bit, I'm sure"; and up went Baden-Powell to the piano, as if obeying an order. In a few minutes the whole place was in a roar, and, as one of the officers told me, the regiment recognised that in B.-P. they had got "a born buffoon, but a devilish clever fellow."

Concerning B.-P. as an actor, it is characteristic of the thoroughness with which he does everything that he always draws and redraws any character he may be playing until he is perfectly satisfied with the dress and make-up; some of these drawings have been captured by his brother-officers, and are greatly treasured.

Soon after joining he began to show his quality as a sportsman. In that regiment of fine riders it has always been hard to shine at polo or tent-pegging, or heads-and-posts, but there was no mistaking the perfect horseman in B.-P. when he got into the saddle, with the eyes of the regiment upon him. Few men ride more gracefully. His seat, of course, is entirely free from that ramrod stiffness which some of the Irregular Cavalry cultivate with such painful assiduity; he sits easily and gracefully, so easily that you might fancy a rough horse would set him bobbing and slipping like a cockney astride a donkey on the sands. But with all the ease and grace, there is strength there, such as would wear down the nastiest of bad brutes. The leg that looks so lightly and gracefully posed grips like steel, and the pressure increases relentlessly the more the horse quarrels with his rider. Many a time has Baden-Powell taken in hand young horses which have defied the efforts of the rough-riding Sergeant-Major, and so far as I can gather there was never a case of the horse beating the rider. His skill as a breaker of horses deserves especial mention because of the characteristic manner in which it is done. By simply sticking in the saddle, and gripping with his legs, he wears down the horse's opposition, silently matching his powers of endurance against the tricks and tempers of the unruly member. Seldom does whip or spur come into play when Baden-Powell is fighting for the mastery with an undisciplined horse.

But while he was proving himself a good sportsman, B.-P. was getting to know about soldiering, paying great attention to regimental work and loyally working to please his captains. Not only did he devote himself to the ordinary routine of regimental work, but in spare moments he began to read up special subjects, and it seems only natural that one of the first of these subjects should be Topography. The result of this labour was that in 1878 Baden-Powell passed the Garrison Class, taking a First Class and Extra Certificate (Star) for Topography. During the lectures he distinguished himself by making inimitable caricatures, for which he was sometimes taken to task by the authorities. Also he could not help poking fun at the examiners in the papers themselves. Asked, "Do you know why so-and-so, and so-and-so?" Baden-Powell would write an interrogative "No."

After distinguishing himself in this way, B.-P. came back to England, in order to go through the Musketry Course at Hythe. Here he did equally well, taking a First Class Extra Certificate, and a year after we find him as Musketry Instructor at Quetta. But this book is not intended to be a "biography" of Baden-Powell, and I shall beg leave to relate no chronological record of his military career. We are telling his story as a story, hoping to interest every English schoolboy who has arrived at years of discretion, hoping to make them keen on sport, keen on exercise, keen on open-air life, and hoping, in addition, to be of real practical use to those whose eyes are now set hungrily on Sandhurst.

In a later chapter it will be seen how Baden-Powell interested himself in his men's welfare, and how he encouraged them to become real soldiers—learned in things other than mere boot-cleaning and button-polishing. Here we behold him as the gay and dashing Hussar, a bold sportsman, a keen soldier, and one of the most popular men in India.

His popularity, it is only fair to say, was earned very largely by that gift for acting which had won him fame as a schoolboy. Whispers that he was going to act in the *Area Belle*, or one of Gilbert and Sullivan's operas, travelled with amazing rapidity from station to station in India, and every performance in which he took part was attended by all the Europeans for miles round. Indeed his fame as an actor travelled so far afield that the manager of a London theatre wrote to him in India offering our astonished hero a position in his company at a salary of ten pounds a week! There is never an occasion when B.-P. is not willing to get up theatricals. A few months after the siege of Kandahar he arranged for a performance of *The Pirates of Penzance* in that barbarous city, making himself responsible for the entire management. The dresses were excellent, the stage and scenery good, and the opera was received with intense enthusiasm; and yet there was not a single European woman there; all the dresses and costumes were the work of B.-P., who himself appeared in the character of Ruth! On another occasion, when *Trial by Jury* was to be given, it was discovered at the last moment, to the consternation of every one except B.-P., that there were no Royal arms. In a few hours he produced what I am assured was the most splendid and gorgeous national emblazonry that ever sparkled behind footlights. He had collected a few crude paints from the natives of the district, and had painted the arms with an old shaving-brush. Such is his resourcefulness. And what of his enthusiasm? When he was home in England on sick-leave he sent out to the 13th Hussars the book of *Les Cloches de Corneville*, with excellent sketches of the dresses and hints as to its staging. Again, he has been known to get off a sick-bed in India in order to take part in some entertainment for the amusement of soldiers.

It was shortly after the successful performance of *The Pirates of Penzance*, and after the evacuation of Kandahar, that Baden-Powell very nearly succeeded in putting an end to himself. He was toying with a pistol, in the firm conviction that it was unloaded, when, to his intense indignation, the thing went off and planted a bullet in the calf of his leg. It might have been a more romantically dangerous wound, but it was quite sufficiently uncomfortable. Even now, on any serious change in the weather, B.-P. is unpleasantly reminded of this adventure in far Afghanistan by rebellious throbbing in the old wound.

On his return from Kandahar Baden-Powell was appointed Adjutant and Musketry Inspector to his regiment, and he is spoken of by one who was himself adjutant of this fine regiment for many years as one of the best adjutants in the world. Shortly after this his uncle, General Smyth, Commandant at Woolwich, offered him the tempting appointment of A.D.C., but Baden-Powell preferred India and his regiment, and declined. Life in India suited Master Ste. It provided him with a great deal of real soldiering, much sport, and made him acquainted with one of the most fascinating countries in the world. After he got his troop, he became Brigade-Major to Sir Baker Russell's Cavalry Brigade at Meerut Camp of Exercise, and was appointed Station Staff-Officer and Cantonment Magistrate at Muttra. With all these duties he found time for sketching and writing, publishing *Reconnaissance and Scouting*, and sending many interesting sketches to the *Graphic*. It may not be out of place here to mention that Baden-Powell, among other parts, has played the War Correspondent, working once in that character for the *Daily Chronicle*, and with considerable success.

That Baden-Powell was a marked man early in his career is

attested by the fact of his being chosen as a member of the Board for formulating Cavalry regulations at Simla in 1884. He was eminently a business-man, a managing man, and all his work in the army has been marked by those excellent qualities which go to the making of our great merchant princes. He is shrewd, practical, and what he says is always to the point. His despatches are admirable examples of what such documents should be, never saying a word too much, and yet leaving his meaning clear-cut and unmistakable. For such work he finds a model in the despatch of Captain Walton, who, under Admiral Byng, destroyed the entire Spanish fleet off Passaro: "Sir,—We have taken or destroyed all the Spanish ships on this coast; number as per margin.—Respectfully yours, G. Walton, *Captain*." Says Baden-Powell, "There is no superfluous verbosity there."

But do not let us lose sight altogether of Baden-Powell as the whimsical humourist. There are two stories in the regiment which reveal him in this light very nicely. He was once walking with a friend on the esplanade of some English seaside place, and the day was piping hot. Suddenly, without explanation of any kind, B.-P. sat himself down on the kerb, placed his billycock hat solemnly on his knees, and buried his face in a flaming red handkerchief. This unprecedented sight stirred the depths of the one and only policeman's heart, and he strode valiantly across the road, prepared to do his duty at all costs. Touching B.-P. upon the shoulder with his white cotton glove, the constable demanded, in a deep voice, "Arnd, whaaet's the matter wi' you, eh?" Slowly removing the handkerchief from his eyes, and with a perfectly solemn face, B.-P. explained that he had just at that moment tumbled out of his nurse's arms and that the silly woman had gone on without noticing it. And the other story: being told rather rudely at a picture exhibition in Manchester that he must go back to the hall and leave his stick with the porter, B.-P. walked briskly away, but presently returned, with his stick, hobbling painfully along—a man to whom a walking-stick was veritably a staff of life. The rude official bit his lip and looked the other way.

When the regiment was at Muttra, Baden-Powell lived in a house which boasted a very large compound, and this he dignified by the name of "Bloater Park." At that time it was the habit to speak about men as "this old bloater" and "that old bloater," and the expression so tickled B.-P. that he adopted the name for his lordly compound. Letters would actually reach him from England solemnly addressed to Bloater Park.

Life at this time—if we except the 1887 operations against Dinizulu in Africa, when B.-P. was Assistant Military Secretary, and commanded a column in attack—was for the most part humdrum, and only enlivened by theatricals and shooting expeditions. But B.-P. was ever interested in his men, and planned sports and entertainments for them, which always kept him fully occupied. A friend of his going to call on him in Seaforth, where B.-P. was commanding a squadron, was astonished to find a Maypole in the centre of the dingy barrack square, round which mounted men rode merrily, each with a coloured ribbon in his hand. On questioning the commander, the visitor discovered that there was a deserving charity in Liverpool, and that B.-P. was getting up a military display on its behalf.

Before leaving this subject, let us mention that Baden-Powell was Brigade-Major to the Heavy Brigade at the Jubilee Review of 1887, that he was sent by Lord Wolseley to arrange about machine guns for cavalry use at Aldershot, that he was Secretary to the British Commission at Swaziland in 1888, and in the same year was elected a member of the United States Cavalry Association. One of his most important staff appointments was that of Assistant Military Secretary to the Governor of Malta, where his work for the amelioration of the soldiers' and sailors' lives produced lasting benefits.

His work as a regimental officer will be more fully dealt with in a later chapter.

CHAPTER VI

HUNTER

"The longest march seems short," says Baden-Powell, "when one is hunting game." Many a time, when he has been marching either alone or with troops, his clothes in tatters, his shoes soleless, and his mouth as dry as a saucer licked by a cat, many and many a time has he got out from under the impending shadow of depression, out into the open sunlight with his rifle,—to forget all about hunger and thirst in matching his wits against nature's. This kind of wild sport has an absorbing interest for Baden-Powell. What he would say if invited to hunt a tame deer, lifted by human arms out of a cart, kicked away from playing with the hounds and pushed and beaten into an astonished and bewildered gallop, neither you nor I must pretend to know; but for that kind of "sport" it is very certain he would express no such enthusiasm as he does for the keen, wild, dangerous sport of the legitimate hunter. He will not seek the destruction of any quarry that is not worthy of his steel; he likes to go against that quarry where there are obstacles and dangers for him, and opportunities of escape for the creature he pursues. He is a sportsman, not a butcher; mole-catching never stirred the blood in his veins.

And while he is hunting animals he is educating himself as a scout. His whole attention becomes riveted on the game he is pursuing; he studies the spoor, takes account of the nature of the country, and makes a note in his mind of any observations likely to be of service during a campaign in that kind of

Harold Begbie

country. It is not the work of destruction itself that makes Baden-Powell a keen sportsman.

In the midst of the Matabele war, just as the weary, half-starved horses which had carried his men eighty-seven miles drew near the stronghold of Wedza, Baden-Powell was exhilarated by a meeting with a lion. In his diary against that date he wrote: "To be marked with a red mark when I can get a red pencil." The incident is well related in his diary and is a characteristic of B.-P. It runs: "Jackson and a native boy accompanied me scouting this morning; we three started off at three in the morning, so that by dawn we were in sight of one of the hills we expected might be occupied by Paget, and where we hoped to see his fires. We saw none there; but on our way, in moving round the hill which overlooks our camp, we saw a match struck high up near the top of the mountain. This one little spark told us a great deal. It showed that the enemy were there; that they were awake and alert (I say 'they,' because one nigger would not be up there by himself in the dark); and that they were aware of our force being at Possett's (as, otherwise, they would not be occupying that hill). However, they could not see anything of us, as it was then quite dark; and we went farther on among the mountains. In the early morning light we crossed the deep river-bed of the Umchingwe River, and, in doing so, we noticed the fresh spoor of a lion in the sand. We went on, and had a good look at the enemy's stronghold; and on our way back, as we approached this river-bed, we agreed to go quietly, in case the lion should be moving about in it. On looking down over the bank, my heart jumped into my mouth when I saw a grand old brute just walking in behind a bush. Jackson could not see him, but was off his horse as quick as I was, and ready with his gun; too ready, indeed, for the moment that the lion appeared, walking majestically out from behind the bush that had hidden him, Jackson fired hurriedly, striking the ground under his foot, and, as we afterwards discovered, knocking off one of his claws. The lion tossed up his shaggy head and looked at us in dignified surprise. Then I fired and hit him in the ribs with a leaden bullet from my Lee-Metford. He reeled, sprang round, and staggered a few paces, when Jackson, who was firing a Martini-Henry, let him have one in the shoulder; this knocked him over sideways, and he turned about, growling savagely. I could scarcely believe that we had actually got a lion at last, but resolved to make sure of it; so, telling Jackson not to fire unless it was necessary (for fear of spoiling the skin with the larger bullet of the Martini), I got down closer to the beast, and fired a shot at the back of his neck as he turned his head away from me. This went through his spine, and came out through the lower jaw, killing him dead."

It was during the Matabele campaign that Baden-Powell came across a fine wild boar, which, he remarks, caused quite a flutter in his breast. "'If I only had you in the open, my friend,' thought I. 'If only you had a horse that was fit enough to come anywhere near me,' grinned he. And so we parted." A graphic incident.

It is in hunting the wild boar that Baden-Powell has a universal reputation as a sportsman. He is good, very good, at all sports, but it is as a pig-sticker that he excels, and stands out clear-cut from the rest. And pig-sticking is the sport of all sports which entail the killing of animals in which we could wish him to excel. Hear Major Moray Brown on the subject of fox *versus* pig: "You cannot compare the two sports together. To begin with, in fox-hunting you are dependent on 'scent.' Granted the excitement of a fast burst over a grass country, and that you are well carried by your horse, the end—what is it? A poor little fox worried by at least forty times its number of hounds. Has he a chance, bar his cunning, of baffling his pursuers? No. Now, how different is the chase of the boar of India! There you must depend on *yourself* in every way, and at the end your quarry meets you on nearly fair and equal terms." Let it be remembered that the boar is an animal of great reputation among beasts. It is a well-ascertained fact, says Baden-Powell, that of all animals the boar does not fear to drink at the same pool with a tiger; nay, a case is on record of his having taken his drink with a tiger on each side of him. In his book on pig-sticking Baden-Powell quotes an exciting description of a battle between a tiger and a boar, a battle which will give English readers a vivid idea of the boar's pluck and doggedness. The narrative is as follows: "When the boar saw the tiger the latter roared. But the old boar did not seem to mind the roar so very much as might have been anticipated. He actually repeated his 'hoo! hoo!' only in a, if possible, more aggressive, insulting, and defiant manner. Nay, more, such was his temerity that he actually advanced with a short, sharp rush in the direction of the striped intruder. Intently peering through the indistinct light, we eagerly watched the development of this strange *rencontre*. The tiger was now crouching low, crawling stealthily round and round the boar, who changed front with every movement of his lithe and sinewy adversary, keeping his determined head and sharp, deadly tusks ever facing his stealthy and treacherous foe. The bristles of the boar's back were up at a right angle from the strong spine. The wedge-shaped head poised on the strong neck and thick rampart of muscular shoulder was bent low, and the whole attitude of the body betokened full alertness and angry resoluteness. In their circlings the two brutes were now nearer to each other and nearer to us, and thus we could mark every movement with greater precision. The tiger was now growling and showing his teeth; and all this, that takes such a time to tell, was but the work of a few short minutes. Crouching now still lower, till he seemed almost flat on the ground, and gathering his sinewy limbs beneath his lithe, lean body, he suddenly startled the stillness with a loud roar, and quick as lightning sprang upon the boar. For a brief minute the struggle was thrilling in its intense excitement. With one swift, dexterous sweep of the strong, ready paw, the tiger fetched the boar a terrific slap right across the jaw, which made the strong beast reel; but with a hoarse grunt of resolute defiance, with two or three sharp digs of the strong head and neck, and swift, cutting blows of the cruel, gashing tusks, he seemed to make a hole or two in the tiger's coat, marking it with more stripes than Nature had ever painted there; and presently both combatants were streaming with gore. The tremendous buffet of the sharp claws had torn flesh and skin away from off the boar's cheek and forehead, leaving a great ugly flap hanging over his face and half blinding him. The pig was now on his mettle. With another hoarse grunt he made straight for the tiger, who very dexterously eluded the charge, and, lithe and quick as a cat after a mouse, doubled almost on itself, and alighted clean on the boar's back, inserting his teeth above the shoulders, tearing with his claws, and biting out great mouthfuls of flesh from the quivering carcase of his maddened antagonist. He seemed now to be having all the best of it, so much so that the boar discreetly stumbled and fell forward, whether by accident or design I know not, but the effect was to bring the tiger clean over his head, sprawling clumsily on the ground. I almost shouted 'Aha, now you have him!' for the tables were turned. Getting his forefeet on the tiger's prostrate carcase, the boar now gave two or three short, ripping gashes with his strong white tusks, almost disembowelling his foe, and then exhausted seemingly by the effort, apparently giddy and sick, he staggered aside and lay down, panting and champing his tusks, but still defiant with his head to the foe." But the tiger, too, was sick unto death, and the end of this battle-royal was that he who saw it emptied the contents of both his barrels into the two stricken belligerents, and put them out of their agony.

It is against such a fierce, resolute, and well-armed enemy that Baden-Powell loves to match his strength and cunning. Mounted on his little fourteen-hand Waler, in pith solar topee, grey Norfolk jacket, light cords, and brown blucher boots, and grasping in his hand his deadly seventy-inch spear, he goes forth to slay the wild boar, with all the feelings of romance and knightliness which some people think vanished from the world when Excalibur sank in the Lake of Lyonnesse. It is a battle whereof no man need be ashamed; in which only the strong man can glory. Many a time has the wild boar hurled his great head and mountainous shoulders against the forelegs of a horse, bringing the hunter to the ground for mortal combat on foot. Many a time has the novice, who went out as gaily and contemptuously as the fox-hunter, returned to his bungalow cut and gored on a stretcher. He who goes up against the wild boar must, in Baden-Powell's words, "have matured not only the 'pluck' which brings a man into a desperate situation, but that 'nerve' which enables him to carry the crisis to a successful issue."

When Baden-Powell returned to India from Afghanistan in 1882, he became an enthusiastic pig-sticker (for reasons which we shall give in our chapter on Scouting), and during that year he killed no fewer than thirty-one pigs. In the following year he killed forty-two, and won the blue-ribbon of hog-hunting—the Kadir Cup. Two years afterwards he wrote and illustrated the standard book on pig-sticking (published by Messrs. Harrison and Sons), which is as famous a book in India as Mr. H.S. Thomas's delightful books on fishing.

Hunting the boar takes place early in the morning and again in the evening, so that men find themselves with nothing to do for the greater part of the day. This time is usually spent in the tent sketching, dozing, and reading, with occasional "goes" of claret cup. But it is characteristic of Baden-Powell that he should give useful advice concerning these waste hours. "If you prefer not to waste this time altogether," he says, "it is a good practice to take a few books and dictionary of any foreign language you may wish to be learning." Again, his character as a thoughtful man may be seen in the warning he gives novices against ill-treating villagers, or allowing the shikaris to do so. "Shouting and cursing at a coolie already dumbfoundered at the very sight of a white man is not the way to clear his understanding." His remark that native servants under cover of their master's prestige will frequently tyrannise over the villagers reminds me of a story which I cannot forbear to tell. A bridge had been thrown over a river in some outlandish part of India, and his work done, the Englishman in charge was returning to more civilised regions. Just before turning his back on the scene of his labours he inquired of a villager whether he was pleased with the bridge. The man expressed voluble admiration for the sahib's great skill, but lamented the high toll that was charged for crossing the bridge. "Toll!" exclaimed the Briton, "why, there's no toll at all; the bridge is free to everybody." But the native still protesting that a charge was made, and saying that a notice to that effect was written up in big English letters, the engineer went down to the bridge himself to investigate the mystery. There he discovered his own servant sitting at the receipt of custom, with a flaming advertisement of Beecham's Pills pasted on to a board over his head, to which he pointed as his authority when questioned by rebellious natives.

Baden-Powell tells an amusing story of an impromptu boar hunt. "At a grand field-day at Delhi, in the presence of all the foreign delegates, in 1885, a boar suddenly appeared upon the scene and charged a Horse Artillery gun, effectually stopping it in its advance at a gallop by throwing down two of the horses. The headquarters staff and the foreign officers were spectators of this deed, and hastened to sustain the credit of the Army by seizing lances from their orderlies and dashing off in pursuit of the boar, who was now cantering off to find more batteries on which to work his sweet will. The staff, however, were too quick for him, and, after a good run and fight, he fell a victim to their attentions, amidst a chorus of *vivas*, *sacres*, and *houplas*."

The pig is a born fighter. From his early infancy he learns the use of butting, and perceives, at an age when civilised piggies are just beginning to root up one's orchard, that his growing tusks are meant for other uses than those of mere captivation. Little "squeakers" have been watched by B.-P. having a regular set-to together, while the older members of their family sat in a pugilistic ring grinning encouragement. Once Baden-Powell managed to secure a baby pig, and kept him in his compound, just as he had kept rabbits and guinea-pigs in England. To watch this squeaker practising "jinking" from a tree ("jinking" is "pig-sticking" for jibbing), and charging ferociously at an old stump, was one of our hero's pet amusements for many weeks.

Although dogs are not regularly used in hunting the wild boar they are sometimes employed for scouting in a particularly thick jungle, and Baden-Powell frequently went to work of this kind with a half-bred fox-terrier. He regards as one of the joys of true sport the bending of animals' wills to his own, and while in this respect the horse ranks highest in his estimation, he is always glad to work with a keen dog. Beetle, the fox-terrier, was just such a dog as Baden-Powell would like; he was quick, full of intelligence, a complete stranger to fear, and moreover he had an individuality of his own. When B.-P. started off for the haunt of his quarry, Beetle would sit with an air of great dignity in the front of the saddle, keeping a sharp look-out for signs of pig. At a likely spot the little dog would jump nimbly from the saddle and plunge boldly into the jungle. Then a sharp yap would reach the ears of B.-P., then a smothered growl, a crashing of twigs and branches, and at last, with a floundering dash, out came the boar, struggling into his stride with Beetle at his heels. "In the run which followed," says Baden-Powell, "the little dog used to tail along after the hunt, and, straining every sense of sight and hearing as well as of smell to keep to the line, always managed to be in at the death, in time to hang on to the ear of a charging boar, or to apply himself to the back end of one who preferred sulking in a bush." And in the end it was a change of climate, at Natal, that killed the gallant-hearted Beetle. He died with a tattered ear, a drooping eyelid, an enlarged foot, and twelve scars on his game little body—all honourable mementos of innumerable fights with the dreaded boar.

As showing Baden-Powell's prowess as a hunter we may mention some of the stuffed animals in the hall of his mother's house, all of which have fallen to our hero: Black Bucks, Ravine Deer, Gnu, Inyala, Eland, Jackal, Black Bear, Hippopotamus (a huge skull), Lion, Tiger, and Hog Deer.

CHAPTER VII

SCOUT

All hardy exercise is good for a soldier, but in pig-sticking Baden-Powell found a sport which, in addition to its effect upon the nerves and sinews, gives a man what is called a "stalker's eye," and that, says B.-P., is *par excellence* the soldier's eye. It was this that made B.-P. an enthusiastic hunter of the wild boar. "Without doubt," he exclaims, "the constant and varied exercise of the inductive reasoning powers called into play in the pursuit must exert a beneficial effect on the mind, and the actual pleasure of riding and killing a boar is doubly enhanced by the knowledge that he has been found by the fair and sporting exercise of one's own bump of 'woodcraft.' The sharpness of intellect which we are wont to associate with the detective is nothing more than the result of training that inductive reasoning, which is almost innate in the savage. To the child of the jungle the ground with its signs is at once his book, his map, and his newspaper. Remember the volume of meaning contained in the single print of Friday's foot on Crusoe's beach." And so he advises officers in India to go with a native tracker to the jungle and watch him and learn from him "the almost boundless art of deducing and piecing together correctly information to be gathered from the various signs found." The importance of tracking, and the art of it, is shown in an interesting story which B.-P. tells, a story which demonstrates the close relationship of hunter and scout. A sportsman in India was out tiger-shooting early one morning, with two professional trackers walking in front of his elephant, and the usual company of beaters behind. As they went along, the fresh pugs of a tiger were seen on the ground, but the professional trackers passed on without so much as a sign of having noticed the spoor. In a minute the beaters were up with the professionals, asking, with Asiatic irony, if they had eyes in their professional heads. To which one of the trackers merely replied, "Idiots! at what time do rats run about?" And then the humbled coolies went back to look at the spoor again, and there they saw, after a close scrutiny, the delicate tracing of a little field-rat's feet over the mighty pugs of Stripes. This rat only comes out of its hole early in the night, and retires long before the Eastern day begins, so that several hours had elapsed since the tiger journeyed that way, and the professional was a better man than the amateur.

Baden-Powell has all the qualifications that go to make a good scout. His eye is as keen as the hawk's, and many a time "by keeping his eyes skinned" he has done useful, if unobtrusive, work. Once he was riding in the night with despatches for headquarters' camp, guiding himself by the stars. Arriving at the place where he thought the camp ought to be, he was surprised to find no sign of it. Dismounting from his saddle, he was thinking of lying up for the night (rather than overshoot the mark) when a distant spark, for the fraction of a second, caught his eye. Jumping into the saddle again, he rode towards the place where the spark had flickered its brief moment, and there he found a sentry smoking a pipe. The red glow of the baccy in the bowl had guided B.-P. with his despatches safely to camp.

But not always does Baden-Powell see what he says he sees. On one occasion in Kashmir he was matching his eyes against a shikari, and the story of the contest is related by B.-P. in his *Aids to Scouting* (published by Gale and Polden, London and Aldershot): "He pointed out a hillside some distance off, and asked me if I could see how many cattle there were grazing on it. It was only with difficulty that I could see any cattle at all, but presently I capped him by asking him if he could see the man in charge of the cattle. Now, I could not actually see this myself, but knowing that there must be a man with the herd, and that he would probably be up-hill above them somewhere, and as there was a solitary tree above them (and it was a hot, sunny day), I guessed he would be under this tree." And when the incredulous shikari looked through the field-glasses he marvelled at the vision of the white man—the herdsman was under the tree as happy as a hen in a dust-bath. The uses of inductive reasoning!

A good instance of Baden-Powell's skill in "piecing things together" is given in the same excellent manual on scouting. He was scouting one day on an open grass plain in Matabelel and accompanied by a single native. "Suddenly," he says, "we noticed the grass had been recently trodden down; following up the track for a short distance, it got on to a patch of sandy ground, and we then saw that it was the spoor of several women and boys walking towards some hills about five miles distant, where we believed the enemy to be hiding. Then we saw a leaf lying about ten yards off the track—there were no trees for miles, but there were, we knew, trees of this kind at a village 15 miles distant, in the direction from which the tracks led. Probably, then, these women had come from that village, bringing the leaf with them, and had gone to the hills. On picking up the leaf, it was damp and smelled of native beer. So we guessed that according to the custom of these people they had been carrying pots of native beer on their heads, the mouths of the pots being stopped with bunches of leaves. One of these leaves had fallen out; but we found it ten yards off the track, which showed that at the time it fell a wind had been blowing. There was no wind now, but there had been about five A.M., and it was now nearly seven. So we read from these signs that a party of women had brought beer during the night from the village 15 miles distant, and had taken it to the enemy on the hills, arriving there about six o'clock. The men would probably start to drink the beer at once (as it goes sour if kept for long), and would, by the time we could get there, be getting sleepy from it, so we should have a favourable chance of reconnoitring their position. We accordingly followed the women's tracks, found the enemy, made our observations, and

Harold Begbie

got away with our information without any difficulty."

In the chapters referring to his work as Sir Frederick Carrington's Chief of the Staff in the Matabele campaign of 1896, we shall see what great service Baden-Powell has rendered the army by his tireless scouting. Here I can hardly do better than quote from his *Aids*, for in this book he unlocks his heart as a scout, and in order to encourage non-commissioned officers and men to interest themselves in the more intelligent side of soldiering (not for self-advertisement) tells us innumerable instances of his own interesting experiences. The chief charm of scouting, of course, is in actual warfare, when a man goes out, sometimes alone and unattended, to find out what a well-armed enemy is doing and how many fighting men are to be expected in the morrow's battle. But just as Cervantes could "engender" the ingenious Don Quixote in a miserable prison, so Baden-Powell in the arid times of peace finds means of enjoying the fascinations of scouting. When out in India he used to spend many an early morning in practising, and he gives the result of one of these mornings in his little book on Scouting, which I would have you read in its entirety. It is a book which has many of the virtues of a novel, and is written in plain English.

The following instance will show you how assiduously B.-P. practises scouting, and will also give you an idea as to beguiling your next country walk.

Ground: A well-frequented road in an Indian hill-station— dry—gravel, grit, and sand.

Atmosphere: Bright and dry, no wind.

Time: 6 A.M. to 8 A.M.

Signs: Fresh Wheelmarks. [Fresh because the tracks were clearly defined with sharp edges in the sand; they overrode all other tracks.]

[This must mean a "rickshaw" (hand-carriage) had passed this morning—no other carriages are used at this station.]

Going Forward. [Because there are tracks of bare feet, some ridden over, others overriding the wheel track, but always keeping along it, *i.e.* two men pulling in front, two pushing behind.]

[Had they been independent wayfarers they would have walked on the smooth, beaten part of the road.]

The men were going at a walk. (Because the impression of the fore part of the foot is no deeper than that of the heel, and the length of pace not long enough for running.)

One man wore shoes, the remaining three were barefooted.

One wheel was a little wobbly.

Deduction

The track was that of a rickshaw conveying an invalid in comparatively humble circumstances, for a constitutional.

Because it went at a slow pace, along a circular road which led nowhere in particular (it had passed the cemetery and the only house along that road), at an early hour of the morning, the rickshaw being in a groggy state and the men not uniformly dressed.

NOTE.—This deduction proved correct. On returning from my walk I struck the same track (*i.e.* the wobbly wheel and the one shod man) on another road, going ahead of me. I soon overtook them, and found an old invalid lady being driven in a hired bazaar rickshaw.

While following the tracks of the rickshaw, I noticed fresh tracks of two horses coming towards me, followed by a big dog.

They had passed since the rickshaw (overriding its tracks).

They were cantering (two single hoof-prints, and then two near together).

A quarter of a mile farther on they were walking for a quarter of a mile. (Hoof-prints in pairs a yard apart.) Here the dog dropped behind, and had to make up lost ground by galloping up to them. (Deep impression of his claws, and dirt kicked up.)

They had finished the walk about a quarter of an hour before I came there. (Because the horse's droppings at this point were quite fresh; covered with flies; not dried outside by the sun.)

They had been cantering up to the point where they began the walk, but one horse had shied violently on passing the invalid in the rickshaw. (Because there was a great kick up of gravel and divergence from its track just where the rickshaw track bent into the side of the road, and afterwards overrode the horse's tracks.)

NOTE.—I might have inferred from this that the invalid was arrying an umbrella which frightened the horse, and was, therefore, a lady. But I did not think of it at the time and had rather supposed from the earliness of the hour that the invalid was a man. Invalid ladies don't, as a rule, get up so early.

Deduction

The tracks were those of a lady and gentleman out for a ride, followed by her dog.

Because had the horses been only out exercising with syces they would have been going at a walk in single file (or possibly at a tearing gallop).

They were therefore ridden by white people, one of whom was a lady; because, 1st, a man would not take a big, heavy dog to pound along after his horse (it had pounded along long after the horses were walking); 2nd, a man would not pull up to walk because his horse had shied at a rickshaw; but a lady might, especially if urged to do so by a man who was anxious about her safety, and that is why I put them down as a man and a lady. Had they been two ladies, the one who had been shied with would have continued to canter out of bravado. And the man, probably, either a very affectionate husband or no husband at all.

NOTE.—I admit that the above deductions hinge on very little—one link might just be wrong and so break the whole chain. This is often, indeed generally, the case, and corroborative evidence should always be sought for.

In the present instance my deductions proved pretty correct. I saw the couple later on, followed by their collie dog, riding along a lower road; but I could not determine their relationship to one another.

Note on Examples I. and II.

Incidentally, the horse-tracks of No. 2 gave me a clue to the hour at which the invalid in the rickshaw had passed that way. Thus: I came on the droppings at 7.14.

Assuming that they were actually 15 minutes old and the horses had walked 1/4 mile since passing the rickshaw, 19 minutes must have elapsed since the passing; *i.e.* they passed each other at 6.55.

On my arrival at the point where they had passed, the rickshaw would now be 23 minutes ahead of me, or about 11/4 mile.

But it is not only on set occasions that Baden-Powell practises scouting. He rarely takes a walk, boards a 'bus, or enters a train, without finding opportunity for some subtle inductive reasoning. Thus he recommends the men in his regiment to notice closely any stranger with whom they may come in contact, guess what their professions and circumstances are, and then, getting into conversation, find out how near the truth their surmises have been. Therefore, dear reader, if you find yourself in a few months' time drifting into conversation with a good-looking, bronzed stranger, this side of fifty, who puts rather pointed questions to you, after having studied your thumbs, boots, and whiskers intently, take special delight in leading him harmlessly astray, for thereby you may be beating, with great glory to yourself, the "Wolf that never Sleeps."

The joy of a walk in the country is heightened, I think, by following the example of Baden-Powell, and paying attention to the tracks on the ground. It would be an uncanny day for England when every man turned himself into a Sherlock Holmes, but there is no man who might not with advantage to himself practise scouting in the Essex forests or on the Surrey hills. The world is filled with life, and yet people go rambling through fields and woods without having seen anything more exciting than a couple of rabbits and a few blackbirds.

The chief joy of scouting, however, is not to be found in what Baden-Powell calls "dear, drowsy, after-lunch Old England." They who would seek it must go far from this "ripple of land," far from

> The happy violets hiding from the roads,
> The primroses run down to, carrying gold,—
> The tangled hedgerows, where the cows push out
> Impatient horns and tolerant churning mouths
> 'Twixt dripping ash-boughs,—hedgerows all alive
> With birds and gnats and large white butterflies
> Which look as if the May-flower had caught life
> And palpitated forth upon the wind,—
> Hills, vales, woods, netted in a silver mist,
> Farms, granges, doubled up among the hills,
> And cattle grazing in the watered vales,

And cottage-chimneys smoking from the woods,
And cottage-gardens smelling everywhere,
Confused with smell of orchards.

Far from our tight little island must they journey for that inspiring spell which turns the man of means into a wanderer upon the earth's surface, driving him out of glittering London, with its twinkling lights and its tinkling cabs, out of St. James's, and out of the club arm-chair—out of all this, and wins him into the vast, drear, and inhuman world, where men of our blood wage a ceaseless war with savage nature. And it is when Baden-Powell packs his frock-coat into a drawer, pops his shiny tall hat into a box, and slips exultingly into a flannel shirt that the life of a scout seems to him the infinitely best in the world. No man ever cared less for the mere ease of civilisation than Baden-Powell.

Harold Begbie

CHAPTER VIII

THE FLANNEL-SHIRT LIFE

In *The Story of My Heart* Richard Jefferies begins his enchanting pages with the expression of that desire which every son of Adam feels at times—the longing for wild, unartificial life. "My heart," he says, "was dusty, parched for want of the rain of deep feeling; my mind arid and dry, for there is a dust which settles on the heart as well as that which falls on a ledge.... A species of thick clothing slowly grows about the mind, the pores are choked, little habits become part of existence, and by degrees the mind is inclosed in a husk." Then he goes on to tell of a hill to which he resorted at such moments of intellectual depression, and of the sensations that thrilled him as he moved up the sweet short turf. The very light of the sun, he says, was whiter and more brilliant there, and standing on the summit his jaded heart revived, and "obtained a wider horizon of feeling." Thoreau, too, went to the woods because he wanted to live deliberately, and front only the essential facts of life. "I wanted to live deep and suck out all the marrow of life, to live so sturdily and Spartan-like as to put to rout all that was not life, to cut a broad swath and shave close, to drive life into a corner, and reduce it to its lowest terms."

This longing for a return to nature in minds less imaginative than Thoreau's and Jefferies' results in globe-trotting or colonisation—according to circumstances,—it wakes the gipsy in our blood, be we gentle or simple, and sends us wandering over the waste places of the earth in quest of glory, adventure, or a gold mine—anything so long as it entails wandering. When it stirs in the mind of the disciplined soldier it turns him into a scout, and drives him out of the orderly-room, out of the barrack square, to wander in Himalayan passes and ride across the deserts of Africa. Baden-Powell is a nomad. The smart cavalry officer who can play any musical instrument, draw amusing pictures, tell delightfully droll stories, sing a good song, stage-manage theatricals—do everything, in short, that qualifies a man to take his ease in country houses, loves more than any other form of existence the loneliness and the wildness of the scout's. Often, he tells us, when he is about the serious business of handing teacups in London drawing-rooms, his mind flies off to some African waste, to some lonely Indian hill, and straightway he longs with all his soul to fling off the trappings of civilised society, and be back again with nature, back again in the dear old flannel-shirt life, living hard, with his life in his hand.

Once, after two months of wandering, he got into a hotel and, after dinner, into a bed. But it would not do, he says; in a twinkling he had whipped the blankets off the bed and was lying outside on mother earth, with the rain beating upon his face, and deep in refreshing slumber. The best of beds, according to B.-P., is "the veldt tempered with a blanket and a saddle." When he is on his lonely wanderings he always sleeps with his pistol under the "pillow" and the lanyard round his neck. However soundly he sleeps, if any one comes within ten yards of him, tread he never so softly, Baden-Powell wakes up without fail, and with a brain cleared for action.

One of the sayings of Baden-Powell which I most like is that which most reveals this side of his character. "A smile and a stick," says he, "will carry you through any difficulty in the world." And he lives in accordance with this principle; and it is typical of the man. Over the world he goes on his solitary expeditions, hunting animals, hunting men, making notes of what foreign armies are doing, what are the chief thoughts occupying the minds of distant and dangerous tribesmen, and he never goes about it blusteringly or with the Byronic mystery of the stage detective. He trusts to his sense of humour—to his smile—first; after that, and only when there is no hope for it, do those hard jaws of his lock with a snap, the eyes light up with resistless determination, and *whir-r-r* goes the stick, and—well, it requires a tough head to bear what follows.

Baden-Powell's friends were amused during the early days of the siege of Mafeking by the complaint of some fellow in the town who had incurred the Colonel's wrath. I forget the exact words of the silly creature's complaint, as, indeed, I forget his offence, but it was something after this fashion: "The Colonel called me before him and, in a dictatorial manner, told me that if I did it again he would have me shot. He then most insolently whistled a tune." The last words I believe to be quite correctly quoted: "He then most insolently whistled a tune." How they suggest laughter! One of Baden-Powell's choicest epigrams refers expressly to this very trick of whistling: "There is nothing like whistling an air when you feel exasperated beyond reclaim." Uncle Toby whistling "Lillabullero" when muddled by his scarps and counter-scarps, and Baden-Powell whistling a scrap from *Patience* to prevent himself from kicking a dangerous idiot out of his presence! "He then most insolently whistled a tune." I recall those words sometimes when I am dropping off to sleep, and they wake me up to laugh. I tell this story not only for its own dear sake, but because it is necessary to remember, when considering Baden-Powell's character, that though he meets you with a smile on his face he carries a stick in his hand to prevent you from taking liberties with his good nature. The best-tempered fellow in the world, and blessed with the keenest sense of humour, he can be as uncompromising a martinet as the sternest fire-eater of old days—*when there is real necessity for it.*

In this flannel-shirt life of his, Baden-Powell has had many adventures, but few, I think, are more interesting in a subdued way than one he records in his diary of the Matabele campaign. I give it in his own words: "To-day, when out scouting by myself, being at some distance from my boy and the horses, I lay for a short rest and a quiet look-out among some rocks and grass overlooking a little stream, and I saw a charming picture. Presently there was a slight rattle of trinkets, and a swish of the tall yellow grass, followed by the apparition of a naked Matabele warrior standing glistening among the rocks of the streamlet, within thirty yards of me. His white war ornaments—the ball of clipped feathers on his brow, and the long white cow's-tail plume which depended from his arms and knees—contrasted strongly with his rich brown skin. His kilt of wild cat-skins and monkeys' tails swayed round his loins. His left hand bore his assegais and knobkerrie beneath the great dappled ox-hide shield; and in his right a yellow walking-staff. He stood for almost a minute perfectly motionless, like a statue cast in bronze, his head turned from me, listening for any suspicious sound. Then, with a swift and easy movement, he laid his arms and shield noiselessly upon the rocks, and, dropping on all fours beside a pool, he dipped his muzzle down and drank just like an animal. I could hear the thirsty sucking of his lips from where I lay. He drank and drank as though he never meant to stop, and when at last his frame could hold no more, he rose with evident reluctance. He picked his weapons up, and then stood again to listen. Hearing nothing, he turned and sharply moved away. In three swift strides he disappeared within the grass as silently as he had come. I had been so taken with the spectacle that I felt no desire to shoot at him—especially as he was carrying no gun himself." It is little adventures of this kind, I think, which most impress one with the romance and fascination of a scout's life.

On his solitary wanderings over the earth Baden-Powell has had many narrow escapes of death, but none so near, perhaps, as that of an excited native who, after an action, told B.-P. with bubbling enthusiasm that a bullet had passed between his ear and his head! Once Baden-Powell came unexpectedly upon a lion prepared to receive him with open jaws, and but for perfectly steady nerves, which enabled him at that critical moment to fire deliberately, he had never brought home another lion's skin to decorate his mother's drawing-room in

London. Another narrow escape occurred during the Matabele campaign, when Baden-Powell was quietly and peacefully marching by the side of a mule battery. One of the mules had a carbine strapped on to its pack-saddle, and by some extraordinary act of carelessness the weapon had been left loaded, and at full-cock. Of course the first bush passed by the battery fired the carbine, and Baden-Powell remarks of the incident, "Many a man has nearly been shot by an ass, but I claim to have been nearly shot by a mule."

It is Baden-Powell's habit to keep in perfect readiness at his London house an entire kit for service abroad. The most methodical of men, he has made a study of this important branch of a wanderer's service, and when he sets out on his journeys he carries with him everything that is essential both for himself and his horse, and packed in such a way as would be the despair of the deftest valet. When the War Office asks him how long he will be before starting on a commission abroad, B.-P. answers, "I am ready now." Everything is there in a room in his mother's house, and Baden-Powell is never so happy as when that khaki kit leaves its resting-place and is packed away in a ship's cabin. And what journeys he has been on Queen's service! Before he was twenty-three he had travelled over the greater part of Afghanistan, and then after seeing most of India, he was in South Africa at twenty-seven, and did there a wonderful reconnaissance, unaccompanied, of six hundred miles of the Natal Frontier in twenty days. He has travelled through Europe, knows the Gold Coast Hinterland as well as any European, and has almost as good a notion as the Great Powers themselves concerning their frontier defences.

This reminds me that Baden-Powell sometimes spends his holidays in visiting historical battlefields and travelling through various countries to see how their defences and their guns are getting along. He is an excellent linguist, and can make his way in any country without arousing suspicions. During some military manoeuvres one autumn (we need not enter into special details) Baden-Powell was wandering at the back of the troops, seeing things not intended for the accredited representatives of Great Britain, who had the front row of the stalls, and saw beautifully what they were meant to see. What he noted on this occasion is regarded by military authorities as very valuable information.

But exciting as these adventures are, they possess no such fascination for Baden-Powell as the life in breeches, gaiters, flannel-shirt, and cowboy's hat—when the mountains infested with murderous natives are blurred by the night, and he is free to steal in among their shadows at his will, and creep noiselessly through the enemy's lines. The Matabele, of whom we shall speak later on, soon got to distinguish Baden-Powell from the rest of Sir Frederick Carrington's troops in 1896. They christened him "Impessa" then, and to this day he is spoken of by the Kaffirs with awe and admiration as the "Wolf that never Sleeps." Silent in his movements, with eyes that can detect and distinguish suspicious objects where the ordinary man sees nothing at all, with ears as quick as a hare's to catch the swish of grass or the cracking of a twig, he goes alone in and out of the mountains where the savages who have marked him down are asleep by the side of their assegais, or repeating stories of the dreadful Wolf over their bivouac fires. This is the life which has most attractions for Baden-Powell, and if he had not been locked up in Mafeking all through those precious months at the beginning of the war, it is no idle guesswork to say that we should have lost fewer men and fewer guns by surprise and ambuscade.

In this flannel-shirt life, however, Baden-Powell is not always on the serious emprise of soldiering. Most of his holidays, at any rate while he is abroad, are spent in shirt-sleeves. His periods of rest from the duties of soldiering are given over to expeditions which carry him far away from the smooth fields and trim hedges of civilisation; he is for ever trying to get face to face with nature, living the untrammelled romantic life of a hunter, independent of slaughterman, market-gardener, and tax-collector. In his boyhood, as we saw, he loved few things more than "exploring," and now he has but exchanged the woods of Tunbridge Wells for the Indian Jungle and the

Welsh mountains for the Matopos.

Happy the man who carries with him into middle-age the zest and aims of a clean boyhood. There is something invigorating, almost inspiring, in the contemplation of Baden-Powell's meridian of life. The fifties which gave him birth seem now to belong to a remote and benighted era; and the blindest of his unknown adorers, if she has bought a hatless photograph, cannot deny that Time's effacing fingers have something roughly swept the brow where she could wish his hair still lingered,—and yet at forty-three, Baden-Powell, Colonel of Dragoons, goes wandering into bush and prairie, striding by stream and striking up mountain, with all the eagerness, all the keenness, all the abandonment of the gummy-fingered boy seeking butterflies and birds' eggs. For him life is as good now as it was with big brother Warington. He is up with the lark, his senses clear and awake from the moment the cold water goes streaming over his head; there is no "lazing" with him, no beefy-mindedness, no affectation and effeminacy. And I cannot help thinking that if the decadents of our day—for whose distress of soul only the stony-hearted could express contempt—would but for a week or two lay aside their fine linen, donning in its place the magic flannel shirt of Baden-Powell, they would find not only a happy issue to their jaundice, but even discover that the world is a good place for a man to spend his days in—if he but live like a man.

Hear Baden-Powell on this subject, and get a glimpse of his serious side, which so seldom peeps out for the world to see: "Old Oliver Wendell Holmes," he says, "is only too true when he says that most of us are 'boys all our lives'; we have our toys, and will play with them with as much zest at eighty as at eight, that in their company we can never grow old. I can't help it if my toys take the form of all that has to do with veldt life, and if they remain my toys till I drop.

"Then here's to our boyhood, its gold and its grey,
The stars of its winter, the dews of its May;
And when we have done with our life-lasting toys,

Dear Father, take care of Thy children, the boys.

"May it not be that our toys are the various media adapted to individual tastes through which men may know their God? As Ramakrishna Paramahansa writes: 'Many are the names of God, and infinite the forms that lead us to know of Him. In whatsoever name or form you desire to know Him, in that very name and form you will know Him.'"

CHAPTER IX

ROAD-MAKER AND BUILDER

King Prempeh was the first celebrity to receive the attention of B.-P. In his capital of Kumassi, which being interpreted is "the death-place," this miserable barbarian had been practising the most odious cruelties for many years, ignoring British remonstrances, and failing, like another African potentate, to keep his word to successive British Governments. Among the Ashantis at this time (1895) the blood-lust had got complete dominion, and the sacrifice of human life in the capital of their kingdom was so appalling that England was at last obliged to buckle on her armour. To quote B.-P. in a characteristic utterance: "To the Ashanti an execution was as attractive an entertainment as is a bull-fight to a Spaniard, or a football match to an Englishman." Even the most coddled schoolboy will appreciate the force of this comparison.

To give a general idea of these cruelties we will quote a vivid passage from Baden-Powell's book, *The Downfall of Prempeh*: "Any great public function was seized on as an excuse for human sacrifices. There was the annual yam custom, or harvest festival, at which large numbers of victims were often offered to the gods. The late king went every quarter to pay his devotions to the shades of his ancestors at Bantama, and this demanded the deaths of twenty men over the great bowl on each occasion. On the death of any great personage, two of the household slaves were at once killed on the threshold of the door, in order to attend their master immediately in his new life, and his grave was afterwards lined with the bodies of more slaves, who were to form his retinue in the next world. It was thought better if, during the burial, one of the attendant mourners could be stunned by a club and dropped, still breathing, into the grave before it was filled in.... Indeed, if the king desired an execution at any time, he did not look far for an excuse. It is even said that on one occasion he preferred a richer colour in the red stucco on the walls of the palace, and that for this purpose the blood of four hundred virgins was used."

The expedition to bring Mr. Prempeh to his senses was under the command of Sir Francis Scott, and Baden-Powell received the pink flimsy bearing the magic words, "You are selected to proceed on active service," with a gush of elation, which, he tells us, a flimsy of another kind and of a more tangible value would fail to evoke. Of course he was keen to go. The expedition suggested romance, and it assured experience. To plunge into the Gold Coast Hinterland is to find oneself in a world different from anything the imagination can conceive; civilisation is left an infinite number of miles behind, and the Londoner is brought face to face with what Thoreau calls the wild unhandselled globe. The message was received by Baden-Powell on the 14th of November 1895, and on the 13th of December he was walking through the streets of Cape Coast Castle, and had noted how well trodden was the grave of the writer L.E.L., who lies buried in the courtyard of the castle.

It was the business of B.-P. to raise a force of natives, and to proceed with this little army as soon as possible in front of the expedition, acting as a covering force. That is to say, the work of these undrilled, stupid, and not over-brave natives was scouting, a duty which while it is the most fascinating part of a soldier's life is also one of the most difficult. This then was an undertaking of which many a man might have felt shy, but Baden-Powell (the army is full of Baden-Powells) went at it cheerfully enough. On the arid desert outside the castle, which is called the parade ground, B.-P. and Captain Graham, D.S.O., taught these negroes, under a blazing sun, the rudiments of soldiering. In one part of their drill a few simple whistle-signals were substituted for the usual words of command, such as "Halt" and "Rally," and a red fez was served out to the Levy (which in the end amounted to 860 men) as a British uniform. The glory of this "kit," however, was somewhat obscured by a commissariat load which each warrior carried on his head; but there was no heart under those shiny ebon skins which did not beat quicker for the possession of the red fez. The Levy, of course, had its band—a few men who made a tremendous din on elephant-hide drums, and a few more who produced two heart-breaking notes on elephants' hollowed tusks garnished with human jaw-bones. At the head of this force B.-P. and Captain Graham set out on their journey from Cape Coast to Kumassi, a distance of nearly 150 miles, on the 21st of December.

Soon after leaving the coast the little expedition plunged into the bush, and then amid the giant ferns and palms began to appear "the solemn, shady miles of forest giants, whose upper parts gleam far above the dense undergrowth in white pillars against the grey-blue sky." The Levy had now reached the regular forest, the beautiful, awe-inspiring, but, alas, evil-smelling forest. Here it was found by Baden-Powell that, in addition to scouting, his force would have to play the arduous part of road-makers, and, therefore, whenever he came upon a village such tools as felling-axes, hatchets, spades, and picks were requisitioned. But it was no easy task teaching the negroes to perform this labour. The man who was given a felling-axe immediately set about scraping up weeds, while the grinning warrior armed with a spade incontinently hacked at a hoary tree with Gladstonian ardour. "The stupid inertness of the puzzled negro," says B.-P., "is duller than that of an ox; a dog would grasp your meaning in one-half the time." But B.-P. did not despair of his men, neither did he ill-treat them. For three days he worked hard at tree-felling himself, and he only desisted from this labour on the discovery that the sight of his hunting-crop brought more trees to the ground than all his strokes with the axe. This hunting-crop was called "Volapuek," because every tribe understood its meaning, and during the march Baden-Powell found it of inestimable value. "But, though often shown," he says, "it was never used." The men might be stupid, they might be idle, but B.-P. can get work out of the worst men without bullying and without continual punishments.

It is men like Baden-Powell who exercise the greatest power over the negro's mind. When he condemns them for cruelty or stupidity he is quick to protest against the assumption that he is "a regular nigger hater." Here is the secret: "I have met lots of good friends among them—especially among the Zulus. But, however good they may be, they must, as a people, be ruled with a hand of iron in a velvet glove; and if they writhe under it, and don't understand the force of it, it is of no use to add more padding—you must take off the glove for a moment and show them the hand. They will then understand and obey." British rule is only imperilled when men in authority discard the velvet glove altogether, or—what is probably worse still—wear only the velvet glove, much padded, over their flaccid hands.

Just as he encourages Tommy Atkins to learn scouting and the more intelligent parts of soldiering, so he encouraged these negroes, duller than oxen, and made them useful pioneers. Here is his own simple record of the way he got to the hearts of the Levy: "How they enjoy the palaver in which I tell them that 'they are the eyes to the body of the snake which is crawling up the bush-path from the coast, and coiling for its spring! The eyes are hungry, but they will soon have meat; and the main body of white men, armed with the best of weapons, will help them win the day, and get their country back again, to enjoy in peace for ever.' Then I show them my own little repeating rifle, and firing one shot after another, slowly at first, then faster and faster, till the fourteen rounds roll off in a roar, I quite bring down the house. They crowd round, jabbering and yelling, every man bent on shaking hands with the performer."

But Baden-Powell, while humane and nothing of a bully,

knows the value of strictness, as we have shown, and he admits that sometimes it is even necessary to shoot one's own men in order to maintain discipline. He is, however, careful to remark that an extreme step of this kind "should be the result only of deliberate and fair consideration of the case." "Strict justice," he adds, "goes a very long way towards bringing natives under discipline."

By these methods B.-P. won the confidence of his troops, and under him these rough tribesmen, half-devil and half-child, manfully fought their way through the jungle of forest, cheered by his encouragement, awed by "Volapuek," and gradually growing to respect the dauntless courage of the white man who managed them so nicely. A description of an average day's work will give you an idea of Baden-Powell's task, and the way in which his negroes worked.

Early in the morning, while the thick white mist is still hanging athwart the forest, a drummer is kicked out of bed by a white foot and bidden to sound "Reveille." Then there is a din of elephant-tusk horns and the clatter of the elephant-hide drums. The camp is astir, and it all seems as if the men are as smart and as disciplined as their brother warriors in Aldershot or Shorncliffe. But the negroes have only risen thus readily in order to light their fires and settle down to a lusty breakfast of plantains. After his tub, his quinine and tea, Baden-Powell sends for King Matikoli and demands to know why his three hundred Krobo are not on parade. His Majesty smiles and explains to the white chief that he is suffering from rheumatism in the shoulder, and therefore he, and consequently his tribe, cannot march that day. Baden-Powell, with his contradictory smile, solemnly produces a Cockle's pill (Colonel Burnaby's *vade mecum*), hands it to the monarch, and remarks that if his tribe are not on the march in five minutes he will be fined an entire shilling. "The luxury," exclaims B.-P., "of fining a real, live king to the extent of one shilling." The king goes away for five minutes, and then returns with the intelligence that if the white chief will provide his men with some salt to eat with their "chop" (food) he really thinks they will be able to march that day. B.-P. expresses a feverish desire to oblige His Majesty, and proceeds with great alacrity to cut a beautifully lithe and whippy cane. In an instant that tribe is marching forward with their commissariat loads upon their heads. But there are others still to be dealt with. The captains of one tribe are discussing the situation, and would like Baden-Powell to hear their views. Baden-Powell treats them as Lord Salisbury, say, would no doubt like to treat the deputations that sometimes come to give him the benefit of their opinions; he looks to his repeating rifle, talks about fourteen corpses blocking the way of retirement, and *hey presto!* the other tribe is swinging down the forest-path laughing, singing, and chattering, like children released from school.

On they march through the heavy forest, a long twisting line of men, until the halt is made at mid-day for two hours' chop and parade. Then tools are served out and every company is set to work. One clears the bush, another cuts stockade posts, a third cuts palm-leaf wattle, a fourth digs stockade holes, and a fifth is set to keep guard over the camp and prevent men from hiding in huts. By sunset some seven or eight acres are cleared of bush, large palm-thatched sheds are to be seen in long regular lines, while in the centre stands a fort with its earth rampart bound up by stockade and wattle, and having in its interior two huts, one for hospital and one for storehouse. Besides this the natives bridged innumerable streams and dug and drained roads wherever necessary.

This work can only be seen in its true perspective when the character of the country is borne in mind. For nearly all of its 150 miles the road from Cape Coast to Kumassi leads through heavy primeval forest. "The thick foliage of the trees, interlaced high overhead, causes a deep, dank gloom, through which the sun seldom penetrates. The path winds among the tree stems and bush, now through mud and morass, now over steep ascent or deep ravine." And, in addition to the difficulties of locomotion, there was the haunting menace of the heavy dews and mists which come at night laden with the poison of malaria.

Harold Begbie

But all these difficulties were met with cheerful courage, and though Captain Graham and two other officers subsequently attached to the covering force were incapacitated by fever, the Native Levy fought its way to Kumassi, and won the admiration of all military authorities. It was at Kumassi on 17th January, and though no actual fighting had taken place, the march may be reckoned an achievement of which all Englishmen can be proud.

One incident of the march will have a romantic attraction for those who have sons and brothers doing the Empire's work in distant lands. As the Native Levy with its two white officers journeyed through the bush they came now and then upon bridges over streams and causeways over swamps, all in course of construction at the hands of natives under the direction of a few ever-travelling, hard-worked white superintendents. "Here we meet one gaunt and yellow. Surely we have seen that eye and brow before, although the beard and solar topee do much to disguise the man. His necktie of faded 'Old Carthusian' colours makes suspicion a certainty, and once again old school-fellows are flung together for an hour to talk in an African swamp of old times in English playing-fields." For an hour in an African swamp! and then on again through the never-ending dark green aisles towards the savages smitten with the blood-lust in "the death-place."

The Ashantis did not show fight, and King Prempeh, sucking a huge nut, surrounded by court-criers and fly-catchers, with three dwarfs dancing in front of his throne, consented humbly and meekly to receive the soldiers of the Queen. After Sir Francis Scott had presented Prempeh with his ultimatum the meeting broke up for the night, but the "Wolf that never Sleeps" was on the look-out with his Native Levy for a possible surprise, or for His Majesty's escape. You can imagine how "Sherlock Holmes," as Burnham the American scout calls our hero, enjoyed that work. In the quiet night, under the white stars, a council was being held in the savage king's palace, and B.-P. "shadowed" that regal hut with eyes and ears alive. At three o'clock in the morning a white light streamed out of the palace doorway, and through the clinging mist went a string of white-robed figures, one of them the queen-mother. This little company passed within twenty yards of B.-P., and it was followed stealthily by him until the queen's residence, not hitherto known, was marked down. Then the watchers returned to their ambush outside the palace, and caught a councillor who was stealing away in the night. Almost immediately after this gentleman had been made prisoner two fast-footed men came upon the scene. They evidently suspected something, for they suddenly pulled up and stood listening intently. One of them was within arm's length of Baden-Powell. Quietly B.-P. stood up. The man did not move. A moment's pause, and then, quick as a flash of lightning, Baden-Powell had gripped him, and had, moreover, got hold of the gun he was carrying. Then the patrol came up, the Ashanti was pinned, and, as B.-P. concludes the narrative, "a handsome knife in a leopard-skin scabbard was added to our spoil."

After the palace had been searched and the whole of the fetish village had been burned to the ground, Prempeh, with B.-P. to look after him, set out for Cape Coast Castle. The bitterness to a soldier of that return journey, without a shot having been fired, can hardly be imagined by a civilian, and would certainly be strongly reprehended by those who regard the justest war with horror and aversion. The soldiers had set out on that dreadful march through swamp, and bush, and forest, to fight and bring to the dust a cruel bloodthirsty nation of savages, contemptuously described by Baden-Powell as "the bully tribe" of the Gold Coast Hinterland. Instead of finding the bully as willing to fight as Cuff was willing to face dear old Dobbin, B.-P. found a cowering, cringing enemy, willing to lick the dust and abase himself in any manner the ingenious white man might suggest. So it was with no feelings of elation that the man who had received the pink flimsy ordering him on active service, who had raised and organised the Native Levy, who had cut a road through the bush and forest, draining roads and bridging streams,—turned his back on Kumassi, and marched King Prempeh to the Cape coast. This march of 150 miles was

Harold Begbie

accomplished in seven days. Of this expedition B.-P. recalls "ten minutes' genuine fun,"—that was when a doctor was cutting out from under his toe-nail the eggs of an insect called the jigger, rude enough to make a nest of B.-P.'s big toe. It is such incidents as these that live in the soldier's mind after a hard campaign.

During the whole of these tiresome operations B.-P. of course was hard at work sketching and keeping his diary. He added to his wonderful store of experiences, and had the rare delight of seeing the King of Bekwai "oblige with a few steps"—specially in his honour. But the story of his work—and it is the same with all the quiet work done by servants of the Queen in every part of the Empire—attracted little public notice, and the man-in-the-street had no more idea of B.-P.'s service than the man-in-the-moon. At that time, indeed, few people outside official circles had ever heard of his name, and certainly no stationer would have been mad enough to stick B.-P.'s photograph in his window. Whether Baden-Powell, when he awakes to it, will prefer his present fame to the happy obscurity of those distant days, is a subject for speculation. I could say definitely, if I chose, which condition is preferred by the proud mother of as gallant a son as ever rode horse into the African desert.

CHAPTER X

PUTTING OUT FIRE

A Brevet-Colonelcy was conferred upon Baden-Powell for his work on the Gold Coast,—he was then eight-and-thirty,—and in the same year he was back at regimental work in Ireland. Hardworking as ever, and keen on making his men practical soldiers, B.-P. was settling down to what is called the dull part of soldiering when the gods, in the shape of the heads of the War Office, again interfered with the even tenor of his way. A telegram from Sir Frederick Carrington arrived at Belfast towards the end of April telling our hero that there was to be fighting in Matabeleland, and that there would be room for him on the staff. B.-P. was attending that day the funeral of a man in his squadron who had been killed by a fall from his horse, and after the service he rushed back to barracks, changed his kit, arranged about selling his horses, dogs, and furniture, and just when the English world sits down to its most excellent meal of the day, that oasis of the afternoon desert, he was in a train rushing as fast as an Irish train can rush towards the steamer that sailed for England.

At twelve o'clock next day B.-P. was saying good-bye to Sir Frederick Carrington, who sailed before him, and that done he spent a few miserable days in constant dread that he would be bowled over by a hansom, or catch scarlet fever, and thus be prevented from sharing in the hardships and glory of a campaign. But nothing contrary happened to him, and after affectionate farewells to his family he embarked for Cape

Town on board the *Tantallon Castle* on 2nd May. One of his first labours was to begin an illustrated diary for his mother's delectation, a diary that was afterwards published by Messrs. Methuen in book form under the title of "The Matabele Campaign—1896." The keeping of this diary had its good uses for B.-P.; in what manner he explains in the preface, addressed to his mother,—"Firstly, because the pleasures of new impressions are doubled if they are shared with some appreciative friend (and you are always more than appreciative). Secondly, because it has served as a kind of short talk with you every day." That is the way in which British soldiers go forth to war.

The voyage was uneventful. Drill in pyjamas every morning prevented B.-P. from putting on flesh, and that drill, especially "Knees Up!" seems to have been of a pretty severe kind, for it draws from Baden-Powell the exclamation, "I'd like to kill him who invented it—but it does us all a power of good." That is the saying of the old soldier. In the barrack-room it is considered the right thing to grumble, or "grouse" as it is called, while one is working hardest. Thus the man with a jack-boot on his left arm and a polishing brush in his right hand—going like lightning,—the sweat running down his red face, is the man who swears he ain't goin' to bother about his blooming boots any more, dashed if he is; and after the brushing proceeds to "bone" them violently. The first part of B.-P.'s exclamation reminds me of a friend who says that ever since he arrived at years of discretion he has been searching for the man who invented work on purpose to murder him. He is, of course, the hardest of hard workers.

There were pleasures as well as drill on board: athletic sports, tableaux, concerts, and a grand fancy dress ball. At this ball a lady with a Roman nose appeared as Britannia, but as the peak of the helmet threatened to bore a hole through the bridge of her nose she was obliged to wear her war-hat (as the Hussar calls his busby) the wrong way round. It was probably B.-P. himself who said to the good lady of her helmet, "That is not the rule, Britannia."

On the 19th May B.-P. looked from his port and saw "the long, flat top of grand old Table Mountain" looming darkly against the glittering stars, its base twinkling with electric lights that glinted on the water. That day was of course a busy one for B.-P. as Chief of the Staff, and the first news received by the Man of Mafeking (how odd it seems now!) was that Sir Frederick Carrington had gone up to Mafeking, and that he was to follow. In three days Baden-Powell was in Mafeking, the guest of Mr. Julius Weil, who gave an anxious England as much important news of the gallant little Mafeking garrison during the Boer war as the universal Reuter himself. Odd, too, it seems that while in Mafeking in 1896 B.-P. should write in his diary that "Plumer's force, specially raised here in the South, had got within touch of Buluwayo." Names how much more familiar in 1900!

Buluwayo was the town selected by the Matabele for their first blow, and accordingly with Sir Frederick Carrington and two other officers B.-P. set out from Mafeking on the 23rd May in a ramshackle coach, drawn by ten mules, on a drive of ten days and nights to Buluwayo. On this journey the officers encountered the celebrated King Khama, and it interested B.-P. to find that Khama knew him as the brother of Sir George Baden-Powell, and that he inquired after Sir George's little girl, just as a lady in the Park asks if one's baby has got over the measles. This (if we leave out a dinner at a wayside "hotel," where the waiter smoked as he served our officers) was the one picturesque incident of that jolting, clattering drive of nearly 560 miles, and, therefore, while our hero is groaning in the coach or travelling afield after partridges and guinea-fowl for dinner, we will take leave to look hastily for the reason of his presence in South Africa.

Matabeleland, let us say at the beginning, is included in Rhodesia, a country 750,000 miles in extent, or, so that the size may jump to the eye, let us say as big as France, Italy, and Spain lumped together. This vast country was under the administration of the British Government, but the Matabele, who had been but partially beaten in the taking of their country in 1893, were only waiting their opportunity to throw off the white man's yoke. The opportunity came when the deplorable Jameson raid emptied the country of troops, and left our brave hard-working colonists at the mercy of these savages. But there were other causes contributory to the rebellion. Rinderpest was slaying the cattle of the Matabele by thousands, and the white man's order that, to prevent the scourge from spreading, healthy beasts as well as diseased should be killed was, not unnaturally, quite unintelligible to the Matabele. The rumour spread that the hated white man was killing the cattle in order that the tribes should perish of starvation. The fact, too, that raiding weaker tribes for food was punished by the British further aggravated this "offence." The priests encouraged the spirit of rebellion, and the oracle-deity, the M'limo, promised through the priests that if the Matabele would make war upon the white man his bullets in their flight should be changed to water, and his cannon shells become eggs. Horrible murders followed upon this encouragement, too horrible, indeed, to repeat; but a general idea of the blood-lust which now possessed the Matabele may be gathered from the fact of over a hundred and fifty English people (scattered, of course, in outlying districts) being killed within a week of the M'limo's call to battle. Only a swift blow, then, could prevent the loss of civilisation to South Africa for many years; only a terrible lesson could teach the Matabele that the white man was his lord and master.

Buluwayo, prior to the time of Sir Frederick Carrington's arrival, contained about seven hundred women and children and some eight hundred men. The women and children were accommodated in a laager of waggons built up with sacks full of earth, and further protected from assault by a twenty or thirty yards' entanglement of barbed wire with a sprinkling of broken bottles on the ground. The eight hundred men were organised in troops, and were armed and horsed in an incredibly short space of time.

Outside the town, on the north, south, and east, lay more than seven thousand Matabele, two thousand of whom were armed with Martini-Henry rifles, while the others possessed Lee-Metfords, elephant guns, Tower muskets, and blunderbusses, besides their own native assegais, knobkerries, and battle-axes. This formidable force was further strengthened by the desertion of a hundred Native Police, who took with them to the enemy their Winchester repeaters. Thus it will be seen that all the odds were in favour of the Matabele, but it is only when the odds are overwhelming against him that the Englishman feels he must buck up, and Buluwayo was fortunate enough to possess men of the true breed. Among these let us make special mention of the Hon. Maurice Gifford, who lost an arm in a gallant dash upon the besiegers[1]—a man "for whom rough miners and impetuous cowboys work like well-broken hounds"; Mr. F.C. Selous, hunter and explorer; Colonel Napier, and Captain MacFarlane. These men gave the enemy no rest, and by repeated attacks at last rid the town of any immediate danger of being rushed by the blacks.

Baden-Powell's work when he arrived was almost entirely confined to the office; and working at a desk from early morning to late at night, with no prospect of an early closing movement, began to tell upon his spirits. He became convinced that "our force is far too small adequately to cope with so numerous and fairly well-armed an enemy, with well-nigh impregnable strongholds to fall back on.... Our force, bold as it is, is far too small, and yet we cannot increase it by a man, for the simple reason that if we did we could not find the wherewithal to feed it." If this sort of thing had gone on much longer B.-P. might have learned to look glum for an entire five minutes; but one night at ten o'clock, when he and Sir Frederick Carrington were putting up the shutters of office, into the town rode Burnham, the famous American scout, with news of a large impi of the enemy about three miles outside Buluwayo. This necessitated action, and B.-P. was himself again. With a police-trooper as a guide he rode out to find for himself how matters stood, and, after a hard and refreshing ride, in the early dawn he was able to see the enemy. There they were on the opposite bank of the Umgusa river, their fires crackling merrily, and they themselves apparently as happy as bean-feasters in Epping Forest. Not long after he had caught sight of these fires and the Matabele going backwards and forwards from the water, Baden-Powell was at the head of two hundred and fifty men riding towards the Umgusa. Under the impression, conveyed to them by their sorry old humbug of an oracle, that the waters of the Umgusa would open its jaws and swallow up the wicked white man, the Matebele allowed Baden-Powell to get his force across the stream without firing a shot; but when they found that not only did the waters fail to overwhelm their enemies, but that these same enemies were riding hard towards them, the Matabele took to their heels in order to find cover in some thicker bush. Then the air began to scream and whistle. Bullets flew by the ears of the charging English with a *phit, phit!* and, when they ricocheted off the ground, with a *wh-e-e-e-w!* Up and down bobbed the black heads in the long rank grass, and *bang, bang, bang* went the guns. Some of Baden-Powell's force wanted to dismount and return the fire, but B.-P., without a sword among his men, sang out, "Make a cavalry fight of it. Forward! Gallop!" Then, as the horses raced snorting forward, and the English gave a shout of battle, the Matabele, 1200 against 250, poured an irregular volley into their enemies. The next minute the horses were in among them, flashing by with the lather on their necks, while their riders' revolvers barked angrily in every quarter of the field. The Matabele ran. As hard as they could lick, they bolted like rabbits to their holes, but faster behind them came the avenging English with the velvet glove flung aside and the iron hand visible to their terror-stricken eyes. In the general rout, the mere act of punishment, there were many instances of coolness and bravery. One man got detached from the rest, and suddenly found himself confronted by eight of the enemy. In an instant his horse was shot under him, but almost in the same instant he was standing in front of the eight with his rifle to his shoulder. Before they could close on him with their knobkerries and assegais, or before they could shoot him down, he had used his magazine fire with such deadly effect that four of his enemy were dead and the other four were sprinting for dear life. Baden-Powell had two pretty adventures in this engagement. Having emptied his Colt's repeater, he threw it carefully under a peculiar tree, so that he might find it when business was done; then he went to work with his revolver. As he rode forward he came upon an open stretch of ground, and the first object that struck his attention was a well-knit Kaffir on one knee covering his body with a Martini-Henry. The distance was about eighty yards, and Baden-Powell, telling the story, says that he felt so indignant at the fellow's rudeness that he rode at him as hard as he could gallop, calling him every name under the sun. But the Kaffir was not to be moved even by the best-bred abuse, and he remained kneeling with the rifle pointed at B.-P., until that horseman, with locked jaws and gleaming eyes (those who know him will understand), was only ten yards off. Then he fired, and B.-P. says he felt quite relieved "when I realised he had clean missed me." That nigger was shot immediately afterwards by one of Baden-Powell's men, who was riding to his help from behind.

The other close shave will make the nervous turn cold to think of it. B.-P. had ridden to the help of two men kept at bay by a nigger under a tree, and when the nigger had been killed, he was standing for a moment under the tree, when something moving above him made him look up. It was a gun-barrel taking aim at him. The man behind the gun, standing on a branch, was so jammed against the trunk of the tree as to look part of it, and while B.-P. was making a note of this fact for his next lecture on scouting, *bang* went the gun, and the ground in front of his toes was as if a small earthquake had struck it. That nigger's knobkerrie and photograph are now in the Baden-Powell museum—a museum which began with butterflies and birds' eggs, and now includes mementos of nearly every tribe and animal on the face of the earth.

After the fight Baden-Powell got back to Buluwayo in time for late lunch, and—"made up for lost time in the office." From now it was a case of office for many weary weeks, and Baden-Powell could only at rare intervals steal away for exercise, which he took in the form of hard scouting, sometimes by himself, sometimes with Burnham—"a most delightful companion." His rides with the famous American gave him great pleasure, and each man, both born scouts, learned something from the other. While he was enjoying these expeditions as relaxation from the cramping work of office, he was at the same time picking up valuable information concerning the enemy. During this grind at the office B.-P. used to long for the lunch hour; "it sounds greedy," he says, "but it is for the glimpse of sunlight that I look forward, *not* the lunch." On one occasion his work as Chief of the Staff was so severe that he was unable to leave the office for four days. He was feeling "over-boiled," and got rid of this stuffiness of mind in his own characteristic way. After dinner on the fourth day he saddled up and rode off to the Matopos, spent the night there, and was back in the office by 10.30 on the following day, "all the better for a night out."

All this time the office work increased, and the anxiety of the General and his staff was doubled by reports of rebellion in Mashonaland. The fire of lawlessness was spreading its evil flames in all directions, till reports of murder and outrage covered an area of one hundred thousand square miles, and about 2000 whites found arrayed against them an army of some 20,000 maddened savages.

Fortunately for B.-P. he had in Sir Frederick Carrington a chief who never wastes a man. Excellent as Baden-Powell was in the office (and Tim Linkinwater would not have feared, I believe, to hand the precious Cherryble ledgers over to his keeping) he could render much more valuable service in the field. In the middle of July the reward came for all his independent scouting; he was chosen by Sir Frederick Carrington, as a man who knew the Matopos country and the whereabouts of the enemy, to act as guide to Colonel Plumer—the officer chosen for the immediate direction of operations in the Matopos. With joy B.-P. flung down the pen and took up the sword.

His first move was towards Babyan's stronghold, Babyan being one of the great Matabele chiefs—a chief great in the glorious days of Lobengula—and who now occupied the central and important impi in the Matopos. This work was well done, the enemy's exact whereabouts were ascertained, and the scouting ended in a glorious gallop back to camp after emptying a few guns into a party of savages attempting to cut off Baden-Powell's party. After this came battle.

In the moonlight of the 19th July the little force, nearly a thousand strong, moved out into the Matopos, Baden-Powell going on alone as guide. He went alone because he feared to have his attention distracted by a companion, thereby losing his bearings. There was something of a weird and delightful feeling, he says, in mouching along alone, with a dark, silent square of men and horses looming behind one. So they marched forward, the one incident, and that a sad one, being the killing with an assegai of a dog who had followed the force, and had endangered the success of its movement by barking at a startled buck. The only noise in the column marching behind the lithe, wiry guide was the occasional muffled cough of a man and the sharp snort of an excited horse. When the force was within a mile of Babyan's impi a halt was called, and the men lay down to sleep in the freezing cold night. It was not a long sleep, for an hour before dawn they were in the saddle again, and moving through the darkness as silently as before towards the enemy's stronghold. When the pass was reached which led into the valley held by Babyan the column was prepared for attack, the advance force being under the command of Baden-Powell.

The guide almost jumped with joy, he says, when he spotted the enemy's fires. The fight was to begin. The guns were got up, and in a few minutes they were volleying and thundering, flinging their whirring shells into the masses of Matabele, whose assegai blades glistened in the morning sun. While this opening cannonade was proceeding Baden-Powell found useful work to do. With a few native scouts he started off on his own account and soon found a large body of the enemy elsewhere enjoying a bombastic war-dance, which plainly portended the staggering of humanity and the driving of the British into the sea. Thinking that Colonel Plumer ought not to miss this performance, Baden-Powell sent back word of it, and calling together the Native Levy proceeded to attack the dancers. Their sound of revelry died away, or changed to something more dismal, when Baden-Powell and his men came clambering up the rocky height, leaping over boulders, dodging behind crags, and pouring lead into their astonished midst. With very little delay the Matabele went to earth, tumbling pell-mell into their caves and holes, from whence the rattle of their musketry soon rolled, and where they fancied themselves as safe as a rabbit in its burrow from the attack of an eagle. To add to Baden-Powell's difficulty his Native Levy began to show the white feather, getting behind rocks and wasting their ammunition on the desert crags. Had the Matabele come out of their caves, given one war-whoop, and made a show of descending upon the besiegers, those precious friendlies would assuredly have turned tail and bolted. But the Matabele in the security of their caves made no such sign, and Baden-Powell called up the Cape Boys and the Maxims in the nick of time. In a few minutes the guns were in position on what looked like inaccessible crags, and the Cape Boys shouting and cheering were floundering through bogs, leaping over boulders, and firing with firm hand wherever firing was of use. The fight was now begun in earnest, and B.-P., on a rock directing the movements of his force, was surrounded by the deafening roar of artillery. In nearly every cave on those hills savages lay with rifle to shoulder, finger on trigger, waiting to pick off the besiegers as they came bounding over the rocks towards them. The Cape Boys never wavered; up they dashed, panting and sweating, to the very mouths of the caves, fired their rifles into the darkness, charged in, to reissue in a few minutes, jabbering to each other, and then rushing off to "do ditto" wherever these man-holes existed. Now they were creeping stealthily round rocks "like stage assassins," now leaping forward through the long yellow grass like men in a paper-chase, —always fighting well and pluckily, lifting up their wounded and carrying them to places of safety, and then again joining in the battle, charging without fear upon their maddened enemy, parrying the thrust of sudden assegai with the bayonet that kills almost in the instant that it guards. And while this work was going on, a sudden corner revealed another string of rebels running down a path. "For a moment," writes B.-P., "the thought crosses one's mind, shall we stop to fire or go for them? but before the thought has time to fashion itself, we find ourselves going for them." Again there was the cheering rush, the rattle of rifles, and hard fighting till the enemy was scattered. So the battle went on, and it did not cease until the stronghold was completely cleared. Then the "flag-waggers" signalled back to the main body for stretchers.[2] During this pause Baden-Powell wrote an account of the fighting (illustrated), to be sent home to his mother.

In this manner Babyan was beaten, and the victors went back to camp satisfied with their day's work. On the following morning it was discovered that a column sent by the General to attack the enemy on the Inugu Mountain had not returned, and Baden-Powell with a patrol of a hundred men was ordered to go in search. When the sun was up the little body moved off towards the mountains, and after passing through much difficult country, parts of which were actually in the occupation of the enemy, they struck the spoor of the missing column, and to Baden-Powell's great joy found that the marks were quite fresh and leading outwards from the mountains— showing that the missing men were safe. Very soon after that the patrol was further cheered by seeing the gleam of the column's camp-fires, and after an exchange of events Baden-Powell hurried back to camp to acquaint the General with the good news.

The next morning, forgetting that he had had another night out, Baden-Powell started off for solitary exercise in the mountains, his purpose being to "investigate some signs I had noted two days before of an impi camped in a new place," and to select a position for the building of a fort to command the Matopos. Returning to camp he drew his design and plan for the fort, and in the evening was back in the mountains again with a number of Cape Boys, ready to begin the business of building.

One of Baden-Powell's little relaxations when fighting slackened was the "rounding off" of cattle, a sport almost as exciting as chasing a solitary boar, especially when the cattle are being driven into the mountains for "home consumption" by bloodthirsty and hungry Matabele. On one of these occasions Baden-Powell was wounded. Having rounded off some cattle he was riding towards a party of niggers when he felt a sharp blow on his thigh as though Thor had given him a playful tap with his big hammer. He was bowled over, and thinking that he must have charged into the stump of a tree turned round to have a look at it; but there was no tree. Then he realised that he had only been struck with a lead-covered stone fired from a big-bore gun, and so hopped off like a man who has been kicked on the shins in a football match, to continue the game. No blood was drawn by this bullet, but our hero's thigh was black and blue for many days afterwards.

This was the kind of life Baden-Powell lived at this time as Chief of the Staff. An officer who knows him very well tells me that it is impossible to wear him out; "Baden-Powell," he says, "is tireless." He is keen to be given the most risky and the most solitary work; he can go for days without food and never complains of broken nights. He has an enthusiasm for hard work, and when that work demands cunning of the brain as well as quickness of the hand, as in scouting, B.-P. is as much lost in the labour as a wolf in search of food for its young. Never throughout the Matabele campaign was Sir Frederick Carrington better served than when the young Englishman slunk away into the darkness, and wandered alone and unprotected into the rocky mountains held by the murderous Matabele. And never were those savages more disquieted than when news was brought to them in the morning that the Wolf had been in the mountains during the night.

* * * * *

FOOTNOTES:

[1] After the arm was amputated at the shoulder Mr. Gifford used to feel the pain as if it were in his hand.

[2] Let it not be thought that B.-P. had neglected to bring stretchers. They were brought, but the friendlies who carried them, like the hen that laid the rotten egg, were nervous, and had dropped them in the river, they themselves taking up positions of safety till the fighting was over.

CHAPTER XI

IN RAGS AND TATTERS

Baden-Powell now had what one might term a roving commission. He was sent by Colonel Plumer in charge of a patrol to wander over the vast country covered by the rebellion and see what he could of the enemy, and when found make a note of. It was exactly the work B.-P. liked above all others. There was romance in the dangers of it, and intellectual joy in its difficulties. There was freedom in it, and the glorious feeling that every step he took he was carrying his life in his hand. And not only was life menaced by the bullets and assegais of Matabele lurking in the tall yellow grass, but there was considerable danger, though of a more humorous order, even in the taking of a bath, as B.-P. discovered in going down to a pool and spotting just in time a leering crocodile in the reeds. Lions, too, were stumbled upon in clumps, just as in peaceful England one walks upon a covey of partridges. Then, lying down one day after dinner for a nap, B.-P. discovered on awaking that a snake had selected precisely the same spot for its own siesta. The charm of night marches, too, was occasionally broken by the growling of a bloodthirsty hyaena, following and snarling at the heels of the horses. These were dangers, however, that added the few touches necessary to complete the picture of our smart adjutant of Hussars in cowboy hat, grey flannel shirt, breeches and gaiters, with a face as brown as a Kaffir's, wandering over the South African veldt. During these expeditions, by the way, Baden-Powell's wardrobe came to ignominious grief, and under the tattered breeches, the stained shirt, and the split boots, he was a mere network of holes. The ankles of his socks remained true to the end, but the rest of them, in B.-P.'s euphemistic phrase, were most delicate lace. The one drawback to the tub in the river, leaving out the chance of a stray crocodile, was the difficulty he experienced in getting back into these delicate open-work socks, and the only way of surmounting this difficulty was by bathing—socks and all!

The marches, too, had their intervals of fighting, and the little patrol was frequently so in touch with the enemy that Tommy Atkins and Master Matabele could exchange compliments. "Sleep well to-night," the grinning savages would shout from the hills; "to-morrow we will have your livers fried for breakfast!" And the compliments became sterner whenever the Matabele recognised in the little force of whites the dread "Wolf that never Sleeps." "Wolf! Wolf!" they shrieked with savage ferocity, and if Baden-Powell had the nerves of some of us he must have had many a bad night after hearing that yell, and marking the gleaming eyes and the frothing lips that twitched with lust for his destruction.

Then there was the bitterest work of all. The closing of suffering eyes that had grown so strangely dear during the hardships of such work as this; the saying of farewells to the men who had raced by one's side with Death at their heels for how many hard weeks. Of one of these Baden-Powell writes in his diary: "His death is to me like the snatching away of a pleasing book half read." And solemn as the funeral service ever is, one fancies how awe-inspiring, how poignant its impressiveness, when in the dark, "among the gleams of camp-fires and lanterns, with a storm of thunder and lightning gathering round," a few fighting Englishmen heard its message over the body of a fellow-soldier.

Baden-Powell's description of the day's work at this time gives one a good idea of the life of a patrol. This is what he wrote in his diary for his mother's eyes: "Our usual daily march goes thus: Reveille and stand to arms at 4.30, when Orion's belt is overhead. (The natives call this Ingolobu, the pig, the three big stars being three pigs, and the three little ones being the dogs running after them; this shows that Kaffirs, like other nations, see pictures in constellations.) We then feed horses—if we have anything to feed them with, which is not often; light fires and boil coffee; saddle-up, and march off at 5.15. We go on marching till about 9.30 or 10, when we off-saddle and lie up for the heat of the day, during which the horses are grazed, with a guard to look after them, and we go a-breakfasting, bathing, and in theory writing and sketching, but in practice sleeping, at least so far as the flies will allow. At 3.30 saddle-up and march till 5.30; off-saddle and supper; then we march on again, as far as necessary, in the cool hours of the early night. On arriving at the end of our march, we form our little laager; to do this we put our saddles down in a square, each man sleeping with his head in the saddle, and the horses inside the square, fastened in two lines on their 'built up' ropes. To go to bed we dig a small hole for our hip-joints to rest in, roll ourselves up in our horse-blanket, with our heads comfortably ensconced in the inside of the saddle, and we would not then exchange our couch for anything that Maple could try and tempt us with."

But after months of this hard work, the tireless B.-P. began to knock up. Fever and dysentery attacked him, and he said unkind things to people who bothered him—as witness the message sent to one of the patrolling columns: "If you let the men smoke on a night march, you might as well let the band play too." The justness of the gibe!

B.-P. relates a good story, by the way, of smoking while on guard. A Colonial volunteer officer, Captain Brown, in times of peace Butcher Brown, ordered a sentry found smoking to consider himself a prisoner. "What!" exclaimed the volunteer soldier, "not smoke on sentry? Then where the—*am* I to smoke?" The dignified Captain only reiterated his first remark. Then did the sentry take his pipe from his mouth and confidentially tap his officer upon the shoulder. "Now, look here, Brown," said he, "don't go and make a—fool of yourself.

If you do, I'll go elsewhere for my meat."

To return. B.-P., having lived straight and hard, soon fought down the fever, and in little more than a week was back again at work. It is nice to know that during the time of his being on the sick-list Sir Frederick Carrington went regularly to his bedside and sat for a long time, retailing all the cheerful news of the campaign. Sir Frederick and Baden-Powell, by the bye, are probably the two Imperial officers who know most about South Africa.

During his illness Major Ridley had started off with a column to make war upon the Somabula, and when B.-P. got about again he was ordered to go in search of this force, with three troopers as an escort, and to take command of it. "I could picture nothing more to my taste," he says, "than a ride of from eighty to one hundred miles in a wild country, with three good men, and plenty of excitement in having to keep a good look-out for the enemy, enjoying splendid weather, shirt-sleeves, and a reviving feeling of health and freedom." So the man who had only just got off a sick-bed started for a ride into the forest after Ridley's column, and during the ride the twentieth anniversary of his joining Her Majesty's Service came round and brought its reflections for the diary. "I always think more of this anniversary than of that of my birth, and I could not picture a more enjoyable way of spending it. I am here, out in the wilds, with three troopers.... We are nearly eighty miles from Buluwayo and thirty from the nearest troops. I have rigged up a shelter from the sun with my blanket, a rock, and a thorn-bush; thirteen thousand flies are, unfortunately, staying with me, and are awfully attentive.... I am looking out on the yellow veldt and the blue sky; the veldt with its grey hazy clumps of thorn-bush is shimmering in the heat, and its vast expanse is only broken by the gleaming white sand of the river-bed and the green reeds and bushes which fringe its banks." How could a man feel unhappy with the whole of his wardrobe packed away in one wallet of the saddle, and his larder in the other? Be sure that Lucullus never enjoyed a banquet with the same sharpness of delight as Baden-Powell squatting amid the yellow grass of the veldt with his cocoa and rice.

But there were anxious moments coming for the man who kept on the openveldt the twentieth anniversary of his joining Her Majesty's army with gladness in his heart. After he had found the column and had got into the Lilliputian forest with its stunted, bushy trees and its sandy soil, he was brought face to face with the greatest enemy that can harass, fret, and wear down nerves of steel—absence of water. A commander whose mind is racked by the difficulty, perhaps the impossibility, of finding water for his troops is like the man haunted day and night, waking and sleeping, by debt. "This was our menu," says Baden-Powell: "weak tea (can't afford it strong), no sugar (we are out of it), a little bread (we have half a pound a day), Irish stew (consisting of slab of horse boiled in muddy water with a pinch of rice and half a pinch of pea-flour), salt, none. For a plate I use one of my gaiters, it is marked 'Tautz & Sons, No. 3031'; it is a far cry from veldt and horseflesh to Tautz and Oxford Street!" But this was at a time when B.-P. wrote in his diary: "Nothing like looking at the cheery side of things." The morrow came when he could see nothing but arid miles of sand, when his eyes ached as they ranged the pitiless desert for water; there is no cheery side to that view. Halting his party to give them a rest, he and an American scout named Gielgud started off to make one grand effort to find river or puddle. Hill after hill was climbed to find only a valley of dead, baked grass beyond, and at last, broken-hearted and weary, the two riders turned their horses' heads back to camp. Soon after this the American's head began to bob till the chin rested on the chest, and he forgot the quest of water in the fairyland of dreams. But B.-P. could not sleep, and those keen eyes of his were ranging the desolate country every dreary minute of that ride. And at last he noticed on the ground certain marks which he knew to be those of a buck that had scratched in the sand for water. Overjoyed he got down from the saddle and continued the work of the buck, digging and digging with his lean sunburnt fingers till he came to damp earth, and then—to water. At that moment he saw two pigeons get up from behind a rock some little way off, and leaving his oozing water in the sand he hastened there and discovered to his supreme joy the salvation of his party—a little pool of water.

On this expedition you will be interested to hear that a man who lent valuable assistance to Baden-Powell was your hero of the cricket-field—Major Poore. In the days of the Matabele campaign he had not slogged Richardson out of the Oval, nor driven Hearne distracted to the ropes at Lord's; he was there as Captain Poore of the 7th Hussars, working like a nigger, brave as a Briton, and quite delighted to be soldiering under the peerless Baden-Powell. His fame came afterwards.

During this expedition Baden-Powell gave brilliant evidence of his capacity as a general. He had drawn up a plan for an attack by his own and another column upon a great chief named Wedza, who lived with his warriors in a mountain consisting of six rocky peaks ranging from eight hundred to a thousand feet high. On the top of these peaks were perched the kraals, while the mountain itself, nearly three miles long, resembled nothing so much as a rabbit-warren, being a network of caves held by the burrowing rebels. Wedza's stronghold was steep, and its sides were strewn with bush and boulders; only by narrow and difficult paths was it accessible, and these paths had been fortified by the Matabele with stockades and breast-works. This important and well-nigh impregnable stronghold was held by something like sixteen hundred Matabele—six or seven hundred of whom were real fighting men. Baden-Powell, nevertheless, drew up his plan for the attack, and sat down to wait for the other column which was to act with him. That column never came; only a letter arrived by runner saying that it would be unable to join in the attack after all. "The only thing we could do," says Baden-Powell, "was to try and bluff the enemy out of the place."

So he arranged to win the battle by cunning of the brain. Sending five-and-twenty men to climb a hill which comma-nded a part of the stronghold, with instructions to act as if they were two hundred and fifty, and giving small parties of

Hussars similar instructions regarding the left flank and rear of the enemy, Baden-Powell got his artillery ready to bombard the central position. Just as the five-and-twenty reached the summit of their hill, however, they were observed by the enemy and instantly fired upon. From hilltop to hilltop rang the call to arms, and B.-P. watched through his telescope the yelling savages rushing with their rifles and assegais to massacre his gallant little force of five-and-twenty men under a lieutenant. To create a diversion, Baden-Powell galloped off with seven men to the left rear of the stronghold, crossing a river on the way, and opened fire upon a village on the side of the mountain. By continually moving about in the grass and using magazine fire, B.-P. with his seven men gave the enemy the impression that he had a large army there, and soon the strain was taken off the five-and-twenty on the hilltop. Then Hussars and Artillery joined the five-and-twenty, while a 7-pounder flung deadly shells at every important point of the mountain. Soon after this the enemy made a backward move, and the lieutenant on the hilltop (with the Field-Marshal's baton already in his hand) incontinently began to harry him effectively from the rear.

The end of it was that Wedza's warriors were completely bluffed by the resourceful B.-P.; they were driven out of their stronghold, and the stronghold itself blown into smithereens. During this attack Baden-Powell narrowly escaped death, a small party he was with being fired upon at close range by a number of the enemy hidden behind a ridge of rocks. "My hat," says B.-P., "was violently struck from my head as if with a stick."

This reminds me of the service rendered by Baden-Powell as a doctor. "Three times in this campaign have I taken out to the field with me a few bandages and dressings in my holster, and on each occasion I have found full use for them." Once he doctored some Matabele women and children who had been hit by stray bullets while lying in the long grass. On this occasion he invented what he calls a perfect form of field syringe: "Take an ordinary native girl, tell her to go and get some lukewarm water, and don't give her anything to get it in. She will go to the stream, kneel, and fill her mouth, and so bring the water; by the time she is back the water is lukewarm. You then tell her to squirt it as you direct into the wound, while you prize around with a feather."

After the breaking of Wedza there was work to be done in Mashonaland, and then, when the rebellion had been crushed and the colonist was able to search fearlessly among the charred beams of his homestead ere setting about building anew, the gallant Baden-Powell turned his face towards Old England. Before leaving South Africa, however, he spent the Christmas Day of that memorable 1896 in Port Elizabeth. "After breakfast," he writes in his diary, "to church. Everything exactly ordered as if at home: the Christmas Day choral service with a good choir and a fine organ. And as the anthem of peace and goodwill rolled forth, it brought home to one the fact that a year of strife in savage wilds had now been weathered to a peaceful close."

Then came the voyage across the 6000 odd miles of ocean with Cecil Rhodes, Sir Frederick Carrington, and other interesting people. After that the English coast, and the train to London. And, after that, "through the roar of the sloppy, lamp-lit streets, to the comfort and warmth—of Home."

CHAPTER XII

THE REGIMENTAL OFFICER

I hear you say that Baden-Powell has had glorious chances, that the lot of most officers is humdrum, and that with so much talk about Arbitration and Universal Millennium, you cannot go up for Sandhurst with any certainty that your career will contain a single opportunity for gaining honour and renown. My dear Smith major, believe me, a man may distinguish himself in a barrack square as well as in African mountains or a besieged township. General popularity, it is true, does not come that way; but the opportunity for honour is there all the same, and the distinction one earns on that field has its appreciation in the right quarter. Long before the world of London paraded its streets with portrait badges of Baden-Powell on its heart, or thereabouts, he was a marked and famous man, and before he had drawn sword on a field of battle, or fired a revolver into the yellow grass of the veldt, he was known throughout the British Cavalry as a first-rate, if not the ideal, soldier. It is not a bad ambition, I promise you, to try and be a perfect regimental officer.

A party of sergeants in Baden-Powell's old regiment were once asked by a civilian whether the men liked him. There was a silence for a minute or two, and at last one of the sergeants replied, hesitatingly, "Well, no, I shouldn't say they *like* him"; then in a burst—"why, they worship him!" Let me tell you how Baden-Powell has earned their love.

In the first place, he entered the Army with no mischievous ideas about the manliness and dash of a fast, raking life. That is a great start, for if the soldier despises one type of officer more than another it is the young sprig who affects to consider soldiering a bore, and comes on parade with the evidence of last night's folly and dissipation in his drawn face and dull eyes. Baden-Powell was keen about his work from the first, and never posed as a drawling Silenus in gold lace. In the second place, Baden-Powell, who always possessed a great deal of sound common sense, took an interest in his men, treated them as intelligent beings, and never for once mistook the drunken, devil-may-care Private of fiction for the soldier who goes anywhere and does anything. It is a literary "dodge" to reach the reader's sympathies by drawing the blackguard in order to find the hero; one good deed in that world of unreality wipes out all the unworthiness of a lifetime, and the reader puts down the tale with a longing to fall on the neck and wring the hand of the very next hiccupping Tommy he encounters. As Bishop Blougram says:—

> Our interest's on the dangerous edge of things,
> The honest thief, the tender murderer,
> The superstitious atheist, demireps
> That love and save their souls in new French books—
> We watch while these in equilibrium keep
> The giddy line midway: one step aside,
> They're classed and done with.

This is all very well in fiction, but I protest it is a little hard on the soldier, and it is certainly a dangerous belief for the future officer to grow up in.

The following letter, which appeared recently in the *Daily Graphic*, is well and truly written: "Having served as chaplain of one of the largest recruiting depots in England, may I thank you for your article on the Heroic Blackguard style of literature in vogue just now. Soldiers have often remarked to me that they were represented as 'drunken roughs who couldn't speak the Queen's English.' As a matter of fact, a steadier, better behaved, better mannered class it would be difficult to find. There are exceptions, but not popular exceptions. Blackguardism and heroism very seldom go together, Bret Harte and other writers notwithstanding. The pluckiest and most reliable soldiers are not animated beer barrels, but sober, keen-eyed, sensible fellows, and of such the British Army chiefly consists."

When you are most inclined to think the Private an irresponsible good-for-nothing, look hard at the next Commissionaire you meet on the street. That smart, clean, well-brushed man, with his bronzed face, his bright keen eyes, and general look of self-respect, was once a soldier, and indeed it is soldiering that has made him what you see. Look hard, honoured sir, at the next Commissionaire who comes across your path, and you will never again be disposed to regard the soldier as an insensate good-for-nothing.

"Tommy Atkins," says Baden-Powell, "is not the childish boy that the British Public are too apt to think him, to be ignored in peace and petted in war. He is, on the contrary, a man who reads and thinks for himself, and he is keen on any instruction in really practical soldiering, especially if it promises a spice of the dash and adventure which is so dear to a Briton." It was just because Baden-Powell acted on this assumption in the 13th Hussars that the men learned to "worship" him. The few regular bad-lots that are to be found, I suppose, in every regiment, are certainly no heroes among the rest of the soldiers. The corner in the canteen where they foregather is not crowded, and I have seen them from that unsplendid isolation looking wistfully at the fresh, clean, merry-voiced troopers buying "luxuries" at the bar,—men who are keen soldiers, anxious to excel, and who do not "nurse the canteen."

But bad officers may ruin the best men, and the popularity of the Army with the classes from which its ranks are drawn depends very largely upon the behaviour of our subalterns and captains. No one likes to be neglected, and the great mistake made by so many officers, but never by Baden-Powell, is their apparent indifference to the soldier's welfare "out of hours." In a cavalry regiment, for instance, for the greater part of the year the men have practically nothing to do from dinner-time till the bugle rings for evening stables. Will you believe it, that the commonest way of spending the afternoon in cavalry regiments is by going to bed? Immediately after dinner is over, down go the beds with a clatter, the strap that holds the mattress doubled-up is unbuckled, and under the thick sheets and the dark blankets, minus his boots, the trooper smokes his pipe until he falls asleep. Their officer is with them in the morning, to see that they brush the scurf out of their horses' manes and put the burnisher over the backs of the buckles; he puts his nose into their room at dinner-time to ask if there are any complaints, and withdraws it almost before it is recognised by the men, as if the odour of the Irish stew disagreed with him. After that, unless he walks through the stables in the evening, his men do not see him. Now, how can an officer who soldiers in this dull, stupid fashion ever gain the affection of his men? And, more important question, how can men with such an officer ever grow enthusiastic about soldiering, or even content with their lot?

Baden-Powell devoted himself to the men in his troop, and, when he was adjutant, to the whole regiment. He would get them out of their rooms in the afternoon for sports of some kind, he would encourage them to take up flag-wagging or scouting, and he would work like a slave to provide them with an alternative for public-house and canteen. There is a story about him, which shows how popular he is with the men, and, also, that it is possible for soldiers to take an intelligent interest in practical soldiering. Baden-Powell was delivering a course of lectures, I think on scouting, and every lecture had been attended by a large audience which completely filled the room. Men used to wait outside the door in order to get a seat, just as people stand patiently for hours at the pit-door of a theatre. Among this audience there was one young sergeant who had shown a singularly keen interest in the lectures; he was one of the smartest and cleanest-living men in the station, and had never been charged with drunkenness in his life. At one of the lectures B.-P. was surprised to find the young soldier absent, and he was still more surprised on the following day to find that this irreproachable sergeant was up on a charge of drunkenness. "What on earth made you go and get drunk?" asked B.-P. "Well, sir," said the sergeant doggedly, "I was late yesterday and couldn't get in to your lecture, so of course I had to go and get drunk." He said this perfectly seriously, and there was a very world of meaning in his argumentative "of course."

Baden-Powell was as assiduous in his attentions to his men as any knight to his lady. He wooed them and won them. He did not win by playing to the gallery, asking if they were quite comfortable in their room, and giving them little coddling presents. He won as a man wins a love that is worth winning, by treating the object of his devotion with respect and perfect trust. His work at Malta, when he was acting as Assistant Military Secretary to the Governor, secured for him the affection of hundreds of soldiers and, I am glad to add, sailors too. He was the life and soul of the place, indefatigable in getting up sports and theatricals for the men, and building a permanent club for their use, which effectually prevented the weaker men, or shall we say the more generous hearted? from spending too much money in public-houses. It was a sight to see the gymnasium, in which the theatricals were held, during one of Baden-Powell's performances. The vast floor of the building was crowded with soldiers packed as tightly as sardines, and the rafters running from wall to wall were all bestridden by sailors as happy and as comfortable there as the Governor and his party sitting in the front row in their splendid chairs from the palace. And when B.-P. appeared in the wings a shout such as might have brought down the walls of Jericho shook the great building, and soldier and sailor vied with each other to see who could keep that roar of welcome going the longest. And over and over again did Baden-Powell apply for leave to shirk some great social function in the palace because the hour of such entertainment clashed with the time he spent among Tommy and Jack in the gymnasium or the club.

His opinion of the soldier is a high one, and that is the secret of his success. He loves to recount instances which have come in his long experience, showing the soldier in the best light, revealing his pluck, his love of little children, his chivalrous championing of the weak, his handiness, his humour, his cheerfulness in depressing circumstances, his self-respect, and his honesty. What was it that struck his attention most about the tempting work of searching Prempeh's palace for treasure? That the work which was entrusted to a company of British soldiers "was done most honestly and well, without a single case of looting. Here was a man with an armful of gold-hilted swords, there one with a box full of gold trinkets and rings, another with a spirit-case full of bottles of brandy, yet in no instance was there any attempt at looting." And, eating out his own heart, on that bitter march back from Kumassi to Cape Coast Castle, he had eyes for the splendid doggedness of the British soldier: "In truth, that march down was in its way as fine an exhibition of British stamina and pluck as any that has been seen of late years. For the casual reader in England this is difficult to realise, but to one who has himself wearily tramped that interminable path, heart-sick and foot-sore, the sight of those dogged British 'Tommies,' heavily accoutred as they were, still defying fever in the sweltering heat, and ever pressing on, was one which opened one's eyes and one's heart as well. There was no malingering *there*; each man went on until he dropped. It showed more than any fight could have done, more than any investment in a fort, or surprise in camp, what stern and sterling stuff our men are made of, notwithstanding all that cavillers will say against our modern army system and its soldiers." During that bitter march Baden-Powell asked a young soldier, gripped by fever but manfully plodding on with the rest, whether his kit was not too heavy for him, whereat, says Baden-Powell, he replied, with tight-drawn smile and quavering voice, "It ain't the kit, sir; it's only these extra rounds that I feel the weight of." "These extra rounds" being those intended for the fight which never came.

In the Matabele campaign he was quick to notice the manner in which private soldiers tended some wounded nigger children. "It did one good," he says, "to see one or two of the Hussars, fresh from nigger-fighting, giving their help in binding up the youngsters, and tenderly dabbing the wounded limbs with bits of their own shirts wetted." During that haunting march with the Shangani Patrol, when the rice was cut down to a spoonful, and a horse had been killed to supply the men with food, Baden-Powell found time to note that "the men are singing and chaffing away as cheerfully as possible while they scoop the muddy water from the sand-hole for their tea." And he loves the soldier for all his little oddities. How he laughed over the man who carried skates in his kit through India, and the man in the African desert with a lot of fish-hooks in his wallet! And how he likes to chaff them out of their failings. At Aldershot one of his most popular pieces as an entertainer is that in which he impersonates the barrack-room lawyer. While the audience is waiting for the next singer, there is a noise heard in the wings, and then a loud voice cries, "I tell yer I will go on. It's no use of you a-stoppin' of me, I'm agoin' to tell 'em all about it, I am," and then with a great clatter a private soldier comes bungling on the stage, tunic open, hair all over the place, and cap at the back of his head. "Beg parding, sir," he says to the officer in the front row, "but these here manoeuvres has all been conducted wrong, they have, and I warn't to tell the company how they ought to have been managed. Now if I had had the runnin' of this concern, and not the Field-Marshal, I should have first of all"—etc. etc. The audience yells with delight, and if Baden-Powell really should show up, in his own inimitable fashion, the mistakes of a general (which, by the way, he is quite capable of doing), the audience and the general too, if he is there, laugh all the more.

Men go to him with their private cares and troubles. They know that the man who can make them laugh till the tears stream down their faces, can at the right moment show a serious face, and give ear to the humblest tale of trouble. He makes it his business—and surely it is part of an officer's business—to know all about his men's lives, their families, their favourite sports, their objects in life, and the way in which they spend their leave. When he was in the 13th

Hussars he was always a favourite with the children in the married quarters, and if you could pick out an apple-cheeked urchin playing in the dust of the barracks who did not grin from ear to ear when you asked if he knew Baden-Powell, you had stumbled upon a young gentleman the guest of the regiment.

Baden-Powell even got to learn the names men gave their horses. There was in the 13th Hussars some years ago a handsome little black horse whose regimental number was, I think, A18. To the men he was Smut, and no one ever thought of calling him anything else. One day at stables the squad was called to attention, and the young soldier standing at the head of A18 was mightily surprised to hear a civilian walking side by side with the captain of his troop remark, as he passed up the stable, "Why, there's old Smut!" When the officer and civilian had passed out he turned to the next man, and asked who the deuce the bloke was in the brown hat. "Why, that's Captain Baden-Powell," said the man; and then he added with great pride, "I was his batman once." The young soldier had heard of Baden-Powell before, and was furious that he had not looked longer at him as he passed. An odd circumstance, by the way, concerning the ex-batman. He was a terrible fellow in many ways, always on the look-out for a fight, and in his cups had disabled more than one policeman in the cities where the 13th sojourned. But he kept in his box a little faded red book of quotations, filled with serious and religious thoughts, and he was particularly fond of two of these apothegms: the one, "A prayer is merely a wish turned Godward"; and the other, "A grave wherever found preaches a short and pithy sermon to the soul." He would quote them over and over again in his confidential moments, and, though he might pick out others as he turned the well-thumbed pages of that tiny book, it was always to these two that he returned as perfect specimens of great sayings. And that book, unless I am mistaken, was given to him by Baden-Powell. "If I had been with him right along," he would say, regretting some escapade, "I should have been a sergeant by this time."

Baden-Powell's familiarity with the names of his men's horses reminds one of his difficulty in swallowing horse-flesh during the hungry days with the Shangani Patrol: "It is one thing to say, 'I'll trouble you to pass the horse, please,' but quite another to say, 'Give me another chunk of D15.'" He is a man who can grow very nearly as fond of his troop's horses as of his own.

A good description of Baden-Powell is that versatile officer's own sketch of a man with whom he soldiered on one of his campaigns: "He has all the qualifications that go to make an officer above the ruck of them. Endowed with all the dash, pluck, and attractive force that make a born leader of men, he is also steeped in common sense, is careful in arrangement of details, and possesses a temperament that can sing 'Wait till the clouds roll by' in crises where other men are tearing their hair." The public in the light of recent events will be quick to recognise B.-P. in the latter part of this portrait; I can assure them that the rest is equally accurate. As a regimental officer he exhibits all these good qualities. He can show the men dash and pluck in every sport they care for, his common sense makes him the friend of Tommy Atkins as well as his officer, and the affairs of his regiment are so admirably managed that there is no enervating air of slackness about the barracks from the first monitory note of "Reveille" to the last wailing sound of "Lights Out."

And while Baden-Powell is loved in the barrack-room he is ever the most popular figure in the Officers' Mess. There is nothing of the namby-pamby, I mean, in his solicitude for the soldier's welfare, nothing to make him unpopular with his brother officers, nothing that makes even the youngest subaltern a little contemptuous. *Tout au contraire.* The place he holds in the affections of his brother officers may, perhaps, be seen in a quotation from the letter of an officer in the 13th Hussars, which I received during the most anxious days of the siege of Mafeking. After saying that relief ought to have been sent before, my Hussar says, "Poor dear chap, he must be severely tried. As I eat my dinner at night I always wish I could hand it over to him." Could a Briton do more?

Such then is Baden-Powell's character as a regimental officer. Beloved by the little fashionable world of the Officers' Mess, adored by the men who eat and sleep and clean sword, carbine, and boots in the one room, he presents to the gaze of the schoolboy whose whole thoughts are set upon Sandhurst the beau-ideal of a regimental officer.

To reach that ideal there are five great essentials—keenness, courage, high-mindedness, self-abnegation, humour. Ability to mix freely with private soldiers without loss of dignity is, I take it, the natural gift of a gentleman; and if the officer who devotes himself to his men is high-minded and courageous, always ready to ignore self, with the saving virtue of humour, he will earn not only their respect and admiration, but their loyal and unswerving love.

CHAPTER XIII

GOAL-KEEPER

Baden-Powell was at Henley, preparing to enjoy the festivities of the 1899 Regatta in one of the pleasantest houses on the river, when a telegram arrived calling him to the War Office. This was on Wednesday, and the business the state of things in the Transvaal. On Saturday he was on the sea, sailing away from the coast of England.

As we have said before, Baden-Powell keeps a khaki kit in perfect readiness for emergencies ("he is terribly methodical," says one of his brothers), and, therefore, when Lord Wolseley asked him how soon it would be before he could start, the delighted B.-P. answered with a very enthusiastic "Immediately." But ships are not kept in such easy readiness as kits, and two whole days had to elapse before our hero could set sail for the land where war was brewing. Those two days he spent with his family and in paying farewell visits to his friends. The Old Carthusian naturally bent his steps towards Charterhouse, and sought out Dr. Haig-Brown in the Master's Lodge. "I hope they'll give me a warm corner," he said, gripping the Doctor's hand. And then in a few weeks this Old Boy was in his African corner, enjoying its Avernus-like warmth.

The story of the siege of Mafeking is one of the most interesting an Englishman can read about. One may truthfully say that it is the story of a single man—our hero, B.-P. Good men he has had under him, skilful officers and valorous troops;

but all the daring, all the gallantry, all the heroism would have been powerless in such a situation without the unlimited resourcefulness of the intrepid Goal-Keeper. With a handful of men he has held at bay in a small and very exposed town as many as 6000 Boers, commanded at one time by the dogged and unscrupulous Cronje. And not only this. With his small force he has kept the enemy on tenterhooks all the weary weeks of the siege, sallying out at night to fling his gallant men upon their trenches, storming them in their lines by day, and actually giving the large army besieging his little garrison a taste of cold steel.

In years to come, I suppose, only the imagination will be able to realise the effect on the stoical British mind of Baden-Powell's brisk and witty telegrams. England at that time, let it be known, was in a state of sullen wonderment. Every dispatch brought consternation to our minds. Here were our troops pouring into South Africa, soldiers of renown at their head, regiments famous throughout the world, representing our courage and prestige, and yet check after check, reverse after reverse—no progress, no sign of progress. In the midst of this national gloom came telegrams full of cheery optimism from little Mafeking—a name hardly known then to the man in the street, now as familiar as Edinburgh and Dublin. Who, for instance, can forget the famous message which ran: "October 21st. All well. Four hours' bombardment. One dog killed"? In an instant the gloom was dispelled. In 'bus and tram and railway carriage men chuckled over the exquisite humour of that telegram. Leader writers, unbending, referred to it decorously. The funny men on newspaper staffs made jests about it, and the "Oldest Evening Paper" enshrined it in verse:—

Four long, long hours they pounded hard,
Whizz! went the screaming shell—
Of reeking tube and iron shard
There was an awful smell.

On us they wasted all their lead,

On us who stood at bay,
And with our guns (forgive it, Stead!)
Popped quietly away.

They could not make the city burn,
However hard they tried.
Not one of us is dead, but learn
A dog it was that died.

The reaction was extraordinary. The almost unknown Colonel Baden-Powell instantly became "B.-P." to the general public, and in the twinkling of an eye his photograph appeared in the shop-windows beside those of Sir Redvers Buller, Sir George White, and Lord Methuen. Everybody was cracking jokes about the war, and the Boers seemed to be already under the heel of the conqueror. When men opened their newspapers in the railway carriage it was with the remark, "How's old B.-P. getting along?" The doings of other soldiers in more important positions lost much of their interest, and the public mind became riveted on Mafeking. Here was a light-hearted cavalry-officer locked up in a little frontier town with seven hundred Irregular cavalry, a few score volunteers, six machine-guns and two 7-pounders; against whom was pitted the redoubtable Cronje with one 10-pounder, five 7-pounders, two Krupp 12-pounders, and one Krupp 94-pounder, and probably an army of something like 6000 wily Boers. And yet the Goal-Keeper, 870 miles from English Cape Town and only 150 miles from Boer Pretoria, was as light-hearted and optimistic as a general leading an overwhelming army against a baffled and disorganised foe. Englishmen were quick to recognise the virtue of the man who solemnly sent the death of a dog to be recorded in the archives of the War Office; quick to appreciate the peril of his position; and I do not think I am screwing my string too tight when I say that the safety of Baden-Powell from that moment became a personal matter to thousands of Englishmen all the world over. Miss Baden-Powell at this time was travelling in Scotland, and at some out-of-the-way station she and her boxes detrained. The station-master passing along the platform noticed the name of Baden-Powell on the trunks, and instantly rushed towards her, with beaming face and extended hand,—"Gie me the honour, ma'am," he cried, "o' shakin' your hand." And from this time gifts and letters poured in ceaselessly upon Mrs. Baden-Powell in London, letters from all classes of the nation, costly gifts, humble gifts—all testifying to the giver's love and admiration of her gallant son in Mafeking. One of these presents took the form of a large portrait of B.-P. worked in coloured silks, another a little modest book-marker. And in the streets gutter-merchants were doing a roaring trade in brooches and badges with B.-P.'s face smiling on the enamel as contentedly as if immortalised on a La Creevy miniature. Finally, to complete this apotheosis, Madame Tussaud announced on flaming placards that Baden-Powell had been added to the number of her Immortals.

This, then, was the sudden fate of the man who had returned to England from wandering alone within a stone's throw of the Matabele bivouac fires unknown and unhonoured by the public. I wonder if Baden-Powell had a presentiment of what was to be when, in the early days of the siege, he corrected the proofs of *Aids to Scouting*, and came upon his own words towards the end of that manual: "Remember always that you are helping your *side* to win, and not merely getting glory for yourself or your regiment—that will come of itself."

The wit of Baden-Powell in some measure obscured from the popular view the grimness of his task. Like the true Briton that he is, he considered it part of his duty to make light of his difficulties. But the holding of Mafeking was stern work. The Boers themselves never dreamed the defence would be seriously maintained, and in the early days of the siege they sent in a messenger under a flag of truce offering terms of surrender. Baden-Powell gave the messenger a sumptuous lunch, himself the most delightful of hosts, and sent him back with word to the accommodating Boers that he would be sure and let them know immediately he was ready to yield the town. And to Cronje's humanitarian plea that Baden-Powell should surrender in order to avoid further bloodshed, the Goal-Keeper made answer, one can see his eyes twinkling,

"Certainly, but when will the bloodshed begin?" A little later he got in with a still more irritating piece of irony, addressing a letter to the burghers asking them if they seriously thought that they could take the town by sitting down and looking at it.

But this was at a time when Baden-Powell, in common with the rest of us, believed that the triumphant British Army would soon be coming up to Mafeking, and he himself able to sally out and strike a crushing blow at the besieging force. Weeks passed and the hope died. The Boers cut off the water-supply, and, with contrary ideas of logic, thought that such an action would damp the spirits of Baden-Powell. But that thoughtful and resourceful commander had seen that all the old wells were cleaned, and well filled, so that Mafeking was as secure from a water-famine as it was from the entrance of the Boers. Besides this, Baden-Powell had constructed bomb-proof shelters everywhere, and a boy stood ready with bell-rope in hand to ring immediate warning of a shell's approach. Trenches were dug giving cover and leading from every portion of the town. So perfect indeed were Baden-Powell's defences that it was possible to walk entirely round the little town without being exposed to the Boer fire. Telephones, too, were established between the headquarter bomb-proofs of outlying posts and the headquarter bomb-proof where Baden-Powell and Lord Edward Cecil, D.S.O., laid their heads together and planned the town's defence. And to keep the enemy at a respectful distance, Baden-Powell continually sent out little forces to harass them and keep them in a state of nerves. The Matabele never knew when Impessa was coming, and the Boers could never lie down to sleep with the assurance that they would not be awakened by the rattle of British musketry and the dread "Reveille" of cold steel. Here is one instance. Knowing that the Boers fear the bayonet more than rifle bullets, Baden-Powell determined upon a sortie in which his men should get within striking distance of the large army closing round the town. One night he sent fifty-three men with orders to use only the bayonet, and this insignificant force crept silently to the enemy's trenches in the darkness, and scattered six hundred Boers from their laager. So close to the town were the assaulted trenches of the enemy that the officer's sudden and thrilling "Charge" rang out distinctly on the night to the ears of those anxiously waiting the result of the sortie in Mafeking. This gallant attack completely "funked" the Boers, and at two o'clock in the morning, long after the little force had returned triumphantly to the town, they began another fusillade, firing furiously at nothing for a whole hour. Fight after fight ensued. Whenever the enemy occupied a position likely to inconvenience the town, Baden-Powell took arms against them, and drove them out. After several experiences of this kind the Boer lost his temper, and with it all sense of honour. It is difficult to write without unbridled contempt of their inhuman bombardment of the women and children's laager in the gallant little town which neither their valour nor cunning could reduce. Baden-Powell loves children, and few incidents in the siege of Mafeking could be more distressing to those who know the stout-hearted Defender than these cruel bombardments. His sorrow over the killed and wounded children was of the most poignant character. One of the officers wrote to his mother during these dark days, saying how the whole garrison was touched to the heart by seeing their Commander nursing terrified children in his arms, and soothing their little fears. If anything could have stirred that just and honest nature to unholy thoughts of vengeance it would have been the murder of these children; and I doubt not that he will hit the harder and the more relentlessly when he gets at close quarters with his enemy, fired by the thought of those mangled little bodies and the remembrance of their mothers' agony. And in addition to the murderous shells of the Boers, typhoid and malaria were at their fell work in the women's laager; the children's graveyard just outside the laager extended its sad bounds week by week, and the cheerfulness that marked the beginning of the siege died in men's hearts.

The cheerfulness, but not the determination. Baden-Powell wrote home in December, after some two months of the siege, saying that they were all a little tired of it, but just as determined as ever never to submit. And in order to keep up

Harold Begbie

the spirits of the garrison in the hour when it seemed to many Englishmen that Mafeking was to be another Khartoum and he a second Gordon, Baden-Powell began to plan all manner of entertainments for the amusement of the women and children. The special correspondent of the *Pall Mall Gazette* in Mafeking, who sent to his journal some of the most interesting letters received during the siege, bore witness to Baden-Powell's efforts in this direction. In one of his letters he said: "The Colonel does all in his power to keep up the spirits of the people. To-day we have quite a big programme of events—the distribution of flags in the morning, cricket afterwards, general field sports, plain and fancy cycle races, a concert in the afternoon, and in the evening a dance given by the bachelor officers of the garrison. We have no Crystal Palace or monster variety hall, but nevertheless we manage to enjoy ourselves on truce days, and it goes without saying that the institution of sports and pastimes has done wondrous things in the way of relieving the tension on the public mind, and keeping up the health of the population. It may shock the mind of some cranks to hear that we so spend our Sundays; but if such persons wish to test the worth and the wisdom of a rational Sabbath, transfer them here, and let them have a week of shell-fire. They will speedily become converts." During the Matabele campaign, it may be remarked, Baden-Powell always held divine service on Sunday, and even to those whose training makes them regard the playing of innocent games on Sunday an offence, this holiday of Sunday in Mafeking must surely be regarded as a holy-day, pleasing to the Father of men. The love of Baden-Powell for children, his intense eagerness to keep alive the flame of joy in their young hearts, and the spark of hope still burning in the hearts of their defenders, could not, we may be very certain, inspire any decision displeasing to high Heaven.

Baden-Powell's dauntless courage, his brisk unchanging hopefulness, and his unflinching determination to "stick it out," were the inspiration of the splendid little garrison. To many of them surrender would have meant nothing more than release from a diet of horse-flesh and the irritating confinement of a siege; but no man and no woman in Mafeking even breathed the suggestion that Baden-Powell should haul down his flag; and on the hundredth day of the siege Mafeking sent a telegram of loyal devotion to the Queen, whose anxiety for their safety was not concealed from the world. A hundred days have long since passed, and if the request of Lord Roberts that Baden-Powell should hold out to the middle of May turns out to be history, the siege will have lasted considerably over two hundred days. And during these long, long days men have been in the trenches night and day, children crying to their mothers to be taken away from the pitiless rain of Boer bullets and the terrifying scream of Boer shells; day by day fever has crept in to lessen the number of brave men whose faith in the Old Carthusian never once wavered, and to rob poor mothers of their little ones. And with all these distressing experiences to wear him down and sicken his heart, our hero found himself further hampered by treachery in his own camp.

Treachery it was that frustrated Baden-Powell's great effort to break the cordon pressing so relentlessly upon little Mafeking, and by that means open up communication with those marching to his relief. The battle of Game Tree fort, as it is called, is one of those events which thrill the heart with pride, and then at the conclusion bring tears into the eyes with the reflection that so much skill in the planning, so much valour in the execution, should be defeated by base treachery.

Baden-Powell's plans for the taking of this fort were perfectly understood by his officers. The little force entrusted with the work of carrying Game Tree moved out of the town in the dusk of early morning, and in a few minutes the roar of artillery announced the beginning of a desperate fight. The scream of the engine of the armoured train told the men at the guns to cease firing, meaning that Captain Vernon was ready to rush the position with the bayonet. The scene that followed was magnificent. Waving their hats and cheering like school-boys after a football match, our men started to run through the scrub towards the silent fort. And then as they went, a pitiless fire suddenly poured in upon them, a hail of bullets tore up

Harold Begbie

the ground at their feet, swept down their gallant ranks, like grass before the scythe, and the men realised amid that enclosing and remorseless fire that treachery had forewarned the Boers, that Game Tree was impregnable. But did they waver or turn back? Not them. They were many yards from the fort, and their orders were to storm it. On they rushed, the officers well in front, waving their swords in the air and shouting cheerfully to their men to follow. Three officers, Vernon, Sandford, and Paton, seem to have made a race of it. Through that terrible zone of fire these young Englishmen rushed forward with all the zeal of men striving to be first to touch the tape. Captain Vernon fell ten yards from the thundering fort, and Sandford and Paton were left to fight out that splendid race alone. With a shout from his parched lips, Paton leaped upon the redoubt, caught with his strong hand the corner of a sandbag, jerked it out of position, thrust his revolver through the loophole, and, panting like a man spent, fired into the enemy's midst till he fell, shot through his gallant heart. Sandford, too, had run a great race, and had almost tied with Paton on the post. He flung himself upon the piled wall that could only be broken by heavy artillery, and fell shot through, with his breast almost against the muzzles of the enemy's guns. Nor were the non-commissioned officers and men far behind their valiant leaders; one intrepid sergeant, who was twice wounded, and at some distance from the redoubt, continued the race across the bullet-swept scrub and reached the sandbags almost on the heels of Paton. The men went forward shouting and cheering, unafraid to look death in the face, afraid only to turn back with their faces from the sandbags where the smoke drifted, and from whence the hail of bullets rained. There was no coward among their ranks, and even when the gallant souls realised that the position was impregnable, there was not a single man among them who wavered, or dropped back in the race. From the moment when the order to charge had been given, the attack was an eagerly contested race, with Death sitting on the flaming fort with the crown of glory for their prize.

When an aide-de-camp from the officer commanding the

operations galloped up to Baden-Powell with the woeful intelligence that Captain Vernon had been repulsed, the Goal-Keeper hesitated, and the bystanders saw that he was taking counsel with himself as to whether a second attack should be made upon Game Tree fort. But his decision was soon reached, and in a quiet voice he said, "Let the ambulance go out." And that was the way in which Baden-Powell took the defeat of his great plan for breaking the tightening cordon round Mafeking.

In history are recorded sieges of a more thrilling character than that of Mafeking, but if you consider the story of this little town's defence you will find, I believe, that in few other cases have difficulties of so oppressive a character been borne with greater fortitude and courage. In a large town a siege is not so wearing to the nerves as it is in a little village the size of Mafeking; and in the case of this miniature garrison the troublesomeness has been doubled by the small number of men to share the burden of days and nights spent in the trenches, now blistered by the sun's rays, now drenched to the skin with rain that converted the ditches into small rivers. It is not our purpose to magnify Baden-Powell's defence, but it is necessary to caution you against the natural course of following his example and treating the Boer bombardment as a joke. It was no joke; and, if it had been, even the best of jokes pall when repeated through days and weeks and weary months. But the garrison would never let anybody dream that they were doing heroic things, never send imploring messages for help to men already occupied with the enemy in other parts of South Africa. To the question, "How long can you hold out?" Baden-Powell had only one answer, "As long as the food lasts."

And so we take leave of our friend the Old Carthusian defending his warm corner. As the last page is turned we see him walking through the streets of Mafeking, now glancing with hard steely eye to the forts which throw their coward shells into the women's laager, now turning to give an order with clenched hands and locked jaws, and now stooping down to lift a child into his arms and caress away its little fears. On his mind weighs the safety of that town with its handful of brave lives, the prestige of England, which suffers if the flag once set above the roofs of any town, whatever the size, falls before the assault of the Queen's enemies, and the thought that far away in distant London the mother who made him what he is, waits on the rack for his delivery. Be sure that never a thought of adding to his own reputation enters the mind of Baden-Powell in little Mafeking, that never does bitterness for tardy release enter his soul, and that all his labour has but one great all-embracing end—the victory of his side. "Play the game; play that your side may win. Don't think of your own glorification or your own risks—your side are backing you up. Play up and make the best of every chance you get."

Choose from Thousands of 1stWorldLibrary Classics By

A. M. Barnard
Ada Leverson
Adolphus William Ward
Aesop
Agatha Christie
Alexander Aaronsohn
Alexander Kielland
Alexandre Dumas
Alfred Gatty
Alfred Ollivant
Alice Duer Miller
Alice Turner Curtis
Alice Dunbar
Allen Chapman
Alleyne Ireland
Ambrose Bierce
Amelia E. Barr
Amory H. Bradford
Andrew Lang
Andrew McFarland Davis
Andy Adams
Angela Brazil
Anna Alice Chapin
Anna Sewell
Annie Besant
Annie Hamilton Donnell
Annie Payson Call
Annie Roe Carr
Annonaymous
Anton Chekhov
Archibald Lee Fletcher
Arnold Bennett
Arthur C. Benson
Arthur Conan Doyle
Arthur M. Winfield
Arthur Ransome
Arthur Schnitzler
Arthur Train
Atticus
B.H. Baden-Powell
B. M. Bower
B. C. Chatterjee
Baroness Emmuska Orczy
Baroness Orczy
Basil King
Bayard Taylor
Ben Macomber
Bertha Muzzy Bower
Bjornstjerne Bjornson

Booth Tarkington
Boyd Cable
Bram Stoker
C. Collodi
C. E. Orr
C. M. Ingleby
Carolyn Wells
Catherine Parr Traill
Charles A. Eastman
Charles Amory Beach
Charles Dickens
Charles Dudley Warner
Charles Farrar Browne
Charles Ives
Charles Kingsley
Charles Klein
Charles Hanson Towne
Charles Lathrop Pack
Charles Romyn Dake
Charles Whibley
Charles Willing Beale
Charlotte M. Braeme
Charlotte M. Yonge
Charlotte Perkins Stetson
Clair W. Hayes
Clarence Day Jr.
Clarence E. Mulford
Clemence Housman
Confucius
Coningsby Dawson
Cornelis DeWitt Wilcox
Cyril Burleigh
D. H. Lawrence
Daniel Defoe
David Garnett
Dinah Craik
Don Carlos Janes
Donald Keyhoe
Dorothy Kilner
Dougan Clark
Douglas Fairbanks
E. Nesbit
E. P. Roe
E. Phillips Oppenheim
E. S. Brooks
Earl Barnes
Edgar Rice Burroughs
Edith Van Dyne
Edith Wharton

Edward Everett Hale
Edward J. O'Biren
Edward S. Ellis
Edwin L. Arnold
Eleanor Atkins
Eleanor Hallowell Abbott
Eliot Gregory
Elizabeth Gaskell
Elizabeth McCracken
Elizabeth Von Arnim
Ellem Key
Emerson Hough
Emilie F. Carlen
Emily Bronte
Emily Dickinson
Enid Bagnold
Enilor Macartney Lane
Erasmus W. Jones
Ernie Howard Pie
Ethel May Dell
Ethel Turner
Ethel Watts Mumford
Eugene Sue
Eugenie Foa
Eugene Wood
Eustace Hale Ball
Evelyn Everett-green
Everard Cotes
F. H. Cheley
F. J. Cross
F. Marion Crawford
Fannie E. Newberry
Federick Austin Ogg
Ferdinand Ossendowski
Fergus Hume
Florence A. Kilpatrick
Fremont B. Deering
Francis Bacon
Francis Darwin
Frances Hodgson Burnett
Frances Parkinson Keyes
Frank Gee Patchin
Frank Harris
Frank Jewett Mather
Frank L. Packard
Frank V. Webster
Frederic Stewart Isham
Frederick Trevor Hill
Frederick Winslow Taylor

Friedrich Kerst
Friedrich Nietzsche
Fyodor Dostoyevsky
G.A. Henty
G.K. Chesterton
Gabrielle E. Jackson
Garrett P. Serviss
Gaston Leroux
George A. Warren
George Ade
Geroge Bernard Shaw
George Cary Eggleston
George Durston
George Ebers
George Eliot
George Gissing
George MacDonald
George Meredith
George Orwell
George Sylvester Viereck
George Tucker
George W. Cable
George Wharton James
Gertrude Atherton
Gordon Casserly
Grace E. King
Grace Gallatin
Grace Greenwood
Grant Allen
Guillermo A. Sherwell
Gulielma Zollinger
Gustav Flaubert
H. A. Cody
H. B. Irving
H.C. Bailey
H. G. Wells
H. H. Munro
H. Irving Hancock
H. R. Naylor
H. Rider Haggard
H. W. C. Davis
Haldeman Julius
Hall Caine
Hamilton Wright Mabie
Hans Christian Andersen
Harold Avery
Harold McGrath
Harriet Beecher Stowe
Harry Castlemon
Harry Coghill
Harry Houidini

Hayden Carruth
Helent Hunt Jackson
Helen Nicolay
Hendrik Conscience
Hendy David Thoreau
Henri Barbusse
Henrik Ibsen
Henry Adams
Henry Ford
Henry Frost
Henry James
Henry Jones Ford
Henry Seton Merriman
Henry W Longfellow
Herbert A. Giles
Herbert Carter
Herbert N. Casson
Herman Hesse
Hildegard G. Frey
Homer
Honore De Balzac
Horace B. Day
Horace Walpole
Horatio Alger Jr.
Howard Pyle
Howard R. Garis
Hugh Lofting
Hugh Walpole
Humphry Ward
Ian Maclaren
Inez Haynes Gillmore
Irving Bacheller
Isabel Cecilia Williams
Isabel Hornibrook
Israel Abrahams
Ivan Turgenev
J.G.Austin
J. Henri Fabre
J. M. Barrie
J. M. Walsh
J. Macdonald Oxley
J. R. Miller
J. S. Fletcher
J. S. Knowles
J. Storer Clouston
J. W. Duffield
Jack London
Jacob Abbott
James Allen
James Andrews
James Baldwin

James Branch Cabell
James DeMille
James Joyce
James Lane Allen
James Lane Allen
James Oliver Curwood
James Oppenheim
James Otis
James R. Driscoll
Jane Abbott
Jane Austen
Jane L. Stewart
Janet Aldridge
Jens Peter Jacobsen
Jerome K. Jerome
Jessie Graham Flower
John Buchan
John Burroughs
John Cournos
John F. Kennedy
John Gay
John Glasworthy
John Habberton
John Joy Bell
John Kendrick Bangs
John Milton
John Philip Sousa
John Taintor Foote
Jonas Lauritz Idemil Lie
Jonathan Swift
Joseph A. Altsheler
Joseph Carey
Joseph Conrad
Joseph E. Badger Jr
Joseph Hergesheimer
Joseph Jacobs
Jules Vernes
Julian Hawthrone
Julie A Lippmann
Justin Huntly McCarthy
Kakuzo Okakura
Karle Wilson Baker
Kate Chopin
Kenneth Grahame
Kenneth McGaffey
Kate Langley Bosher
Kate Langley Bosher
Katherine Cecil Thurston
Katherine Stokes
L. A. Abbot
L. T. Meade

L. Frank Baum
Latta Griswold
Laura Dent Crane
Laura Lee Hope
Laurence Housman
Lawrence Beasley
Leo Tolstoy
Leonid Andreyev
Lewis Carroll
Lewis Sperry Chafer
Lilian Bell
Lloyd Osbourne
Louis Hughes
Louis Joseph Vance
Louis Tracy
Louisa May Alcott
Lucy Fitch Perkins
Lucy Maud Montgomery
Luther Benson
Lydia Miller Middleton
Lyndon Orr
M. Corvus
M. H. Adams
Margaret E. Sangster
Margret Howth
Margaret Vandercook
Margaret W. Hungerford
Margret Penrose
Maria Edgeworth
Maria Thompson Daviess
Mariano Azuela
Marion Polk Angellotti
Mark Overton
Mark Twain
Mary Austin
Mary Catherine Crowley
Mary Cole
Mary Hastings Bradley
Mary Roberts Rinehart
Mary Rowlandson
M. Wollstonecraft Shelley
Maud Lindsay
Max Beerbohm
Myra Kelly
Nathaniel Hawthrone
Nicolo Machiavelli
O. F. Walton
Oscar Wilde
Owen Johnson
P.G. Wodehouse
Paul and Mabel Thorne

Paul G. Tomlinson
Paul Severing
Percy Brebner
Percy Keese Fitzhugh
Peter B. Kyne
Plato
Quincy Allen
R. Derby Holmes
R. L. Stevenson
R. S. Ball
Rabindranath Tagore
Rahul Alvares
Ralph Bonehill
Ralph Henry Barbour
Ralph Victor
Ralph Waldo Emmerson
Rene Descartes
Ray Cummings
Rex Beach
Rex E. Beach
Richard Harding Davis
Richard Jefferies
Richard Le Gallienne
Robert Barr
Robert Frost
Robert Gordon Anderson
Robert L. Drake
Robert Lansing
Robert Lynd
Robert Michael Ballantyne
Robert W. Chambers
Rosa Nouchette Carey
Rudyard Kipling
Saint Augustine
Samuel B. Allison
Samuel Hopkins Adams
Sarah Bernhardt
Sarah C. Hallowell
Selma Lagerlof
Sherwood Anderson
Sigmund Freud
Standish O'Grady
Stanley Weyman
Stella Benson
Stella M. Francis
Stephen Crane
Stewart Edward White
Stijn Streuvels
Swami Abhedananda
Swami Parmananda
T. S. Ackland

T. S. Arthur
The Princess Der Ling
Thomas A. Janvier
Thomas A Kempis
Thomas Anderton
Thomas Bailey Aldrich
Thomas Bulfinch
Thomas De Quincey
Thomas Dixon
Thomas H. Huxley
Thomas Hardy
Thomas More
Thornton W. Burgess
U. S. Grant
Upton Sinclair
Valentine Williams
Various Authors
Vaughan Kester
Victor Appleton
Victor G. Durham
Victoria Cross
Virginia Woolf
Wadsworth Camp
Walter Camp
Walter Scott
Washington Irving
Wilbur Lawton
Wilkie Collins
Willa Cather
Willard F. Baker
William Dean Howells
William le Queux
W. Makepeace Thackeray
William W. Walter
William Shakespeare
Winston Churchill
Yei Theodora Ozaki
Yogi Ramacharaka
Young E. Allison
Zane Grey

www.ingramcontent.com/pod-product-compliance
Lightning Source LLC
Chambersburg PA
CBHW032008040426
42448CB00006B/543